Falling but Fulfilled
Reflections on Multiple Intelligences

by

Zachary M. Oliver

Savant Books and Publications
Honolulu, HI
2010

Published in the USA by Savant Books and Publications
2630 Kapiolani Blvd #1601
Honolulu, HI 96826
http://www.savantbooksandpublications.com

Printed in the USA

Edited by Jonathan Marcantoni
Cover by Daniel S. Janik

Copyright 2010 Zachary M. Oliver. All rights reserved. No part of this work may be reproduced without the prior written permission of the author.

13-digit ISBN: 978-0-9845552-7-7
10-digit ISBN: 0-9845552-7-7

This book is primarily non-fictional; though the information conveyed comes from different sources, every effort has been made to make this work as accurate as possible. However, there may remain mistakes, both typographical and in content. Information conveyed is current up to the printing date.

The author and publisher have neither liability nor responsibility to any person or entity with respect to any loss or damage caused, or alleged to have been caused, directly or indirectly, by the information conveyed in this book.

Howard Gardner has kindly reviewed this work.

Dedication

To Danpoong:
Let the rice blossoms dance in the breeze...

Acknowledgements

A peek behind the curtain:

First, I'd like to acknowledge Dr. Howard Gardner, Hobb's Professor of Cognition and Education at Harvard University for the Multiple Intelligences (MI) Theory. Twenty-five years after its birth, MI theory, originally put forth in his fascinating book, "Frames of Mind," is still a beautiful and elegant perspective on intelligence. With this theory, Dr. Gardner started a conversation that cuts across education, psychology, and business. Without his contributions, this book would not exist. Thank you, Dr. Gardner, for reading this manuscript and providing the comment for the cover.

Next, I want to acknowledge Drs. Jack Mezirow, Brett Cameron, and Daniel S. Janik whose contributions to Transformative Learning Theory provided a large textural influence on the style which I chose (along with some perfectly-timed prodding by my amazing editor, Jon Marcantoni) to write this book. My first impulse was to write an academic work full of big words discussing the idea of MI Theory. Luckily, this impulse just didn't feel right. After all, most academicians already know of Dr. Gardner's work. I wanted to write to a larger audience: Those who were actually engaged in learning—students, parents, educators and researchers alike. I had just completed reading Dr. Mezirow's "Learning as Transformation," Dr. Cameron's "SelfDesign," and Dr. Janik's "Unlock the Genius Within," and I began to think about the centrality of critical reflection as a key in the transformative process of learning. I recognized that education should be transformative in a way that I'd always felt, but never heard or experienced during my formal education. What struck me in particular was that transformations don't just happen; the stage has to be set, and critical reflection is an essential part of that preparation. After numerous discussions with Jon, I therefore decided to write this book as a memoir, utilizing a critical reflection approach, in the hopes that it would open MI Theory to a wider audience.

I'd also like to acknowledge Primo Castro, the fearless heart of an organization, a man near and dear to my heart who first took a chance on me, recognized my talent, and gave me the space and faith to develop to my current potential. I'd like to thank Merrill Cutting for believing in Primo (even though the two held vastly different points-of-view) and for giving me an academic home for so many years. And, Sherry Fieser: Thank you for the late night discussions. You are all "ohana" (Hawaiian for "family") to me. I hope this book feels like an extension of our intellectual work over the years.

A special "Thank You" to my current colleagues: Warren Evans, Chris Catron, Ken Rasti, Rodger Epstein, Pono Shim, Kris and Kenneth Lesperance, Carol Parrington, Gary Krinberg, Kevin Yu, David Stewart, Carole Hope, and Donna Duellberg. Each of you contributed to the heart and soul of this text and I hope you see a part of yourself in it. What you have shared with me still reverberates through everything that I strive for as an educator and, most importantly, as a caring human being.

I am blessed with a wonderful family. Moving from the center outward, I'd like to thank my loving wife, Chung Hea, my beautiful daughters, Natalie and Pahda, my mom and dad, all of whom live in Hawaii: Thank you for inspiring to share the thoughts in this work with the world. Anique and Clemens, Adrianne and Paul, and Jeremy and Christie—you are my "brothers" and "sisters," each having taught me something about myself. You are the stars in my night sky, helping me to navigate my life.

Finally, I'd like to express my appreciation to Savant Publications for offering me the opportunity to find a voice and the mentorship to get this voice onto paper. It's my sincere hope that my students past, present, and future will read this work and see how deeply they have touched me, how their energy and enthusiasm has inspired me, and how their stories have challenged me to tell my own.

~ Zachary M. Oliver (2010)

Table of Contents

Prologue	Page 1
Multiple Intelligences Theory A Forward	Page 7
1-Bodily-Kinesthetic Intelligence	Page 13
2- Interpersonal Intelligence	Page 31
3-Intrapersonal Intelligence	Page 51
4-Musical Intelligence	Page 71
5-Naturalist Intelligence	Page 85
6-Visual-Spatial Intelligence	Page 97
7-Linguistic Intelligence	Page 111
8-Logical-Mathematical Intelligence	Page 123
9-On Motivation	Page 143
10-A Manifesto	Page 153
Appendix: What is Intelligence?	Page 165

"A bio-psychological potential to process information that can be activated in a cultural setting to solve problems or create products that are of value in a culture"
～ Intelligence, as defined by Howard Gardner

Zachary M. Oliver

Prologue

Upon beginning my career as an educator more than a decade ago, I thought that all of the really important questions about how learning occurs, when it occurs, and what needs to be set in order for it to occur had already been answered. I walked into my first teaching experience thinking that I had been taught well. At first, I attempted to re-create my learning experience for my students with few personal touches. Like a thousand teachers before me, my classroom became a galaxy revolving around me held together by my gravitas. While this method carried me through the first couple of years, I soon began to watch more carefully and noticed that my colorful lectures and interactive activities weren't transforming my students no matter how well-planned and executed. Exhausted students sat in front of me day and night doing nothing more than what they had to just to get through the class.

Seizing the opportunity presented by that realization, I scratched my head, walked into the faculty room and voiced a delightfully short-sighted observation about my students' bad habits. Questions came from my mouth asking "Why aren't my students prepared?" "Why do they insist on partying all night on drug and video game binges?" and "Jeez, what's their problem?" Of course, I received a set of knowing looks from a bunch of tired-looking, sad-eyed teachers who, having heard this a million times, quickly tuned back out and returned their focus to the television and their cherished coffee mugs.

Luckily, instead of accepting this status quo that everyone seemed to recognize but not address—this elephant in the room—my conscience got the better of me.

I started asking questions that extended past grammar and sentence structure. Taking the time to get to know some of the students, I found out some interesting things. For example, many of them had children, despite still being in their teens. I found out that they worked all day and came to school at night. Or, they worked all night through a graveyard shift and then pushed through a day of school. Some of them literally slept on public transportation as they moved from school to work, stopping home for nothing more than a bite to eat and a shower. Slowly a realization took root in my mind: This is today's college student population.

These students are willing to push everything to the limit just to try to find a way to improve their lives and the lives of their children. This was profoundly troubling and, at the same time, deeply inspiring. The exhaustion they feel because of the demands placed on them sharpens them in strange ways. These students know when someone isn't authentic. They can tell when someone is not emotionally accountable to their chosen career. The effort put into trying to reach the next level of education, maturity, and opportunity sharpens them to slice through the nice facades we put up and quickly identify who really cares about their growth and who is merely collecting a paycheck.

Over the course of the next couple of months, I felt my eyes burning me in the mirror. Blown away by these realizations, I knew that I needed to respond to these students' output in kind in order to earn the right to be their mentor.

I had entertained thoughts of advanced degrees, but I hadn't found the impetus on my own until I became aware of the adversity these students were facing. Suddenly, my world was upended. I knew that I needed to return to school and push my growth by humbly tapping into their commitment and focus as my example and inspiration. An effective educator has to also be an active learner. How could I call myself an active learner until I had pushed my own formal education as far as possible? I felt that these students deserved a chance for a better way of achieving their wish for an education as well as the opportunities that emerge for those that distinguish themselves through academic success. It became important for me to be a part of that growth by helping to find a way to assist in the struggles each of these students faced in their pursuit of an education.

During my studies, I've studied, adapted, and played with a lot of philosophies, theories, and teaching models. Each has enriched my life and my own experience as a student of this fathomless experience of life. For as many of these philosophies and theories as I have looked at, there are whole oceans of intellectual literature into which I've yet to sail. I've studied, taught, and have administered traditional learning environments, and completely online environments, and I've found myself deeply involved with the challenges of mixing these two extremes, online and traditional, in various blended-model settings. In my guts, I have deeply conflicted feelings about each of these models.

My reasons for writing this book are diverse: I want to share my experiences with teachers who may be feeling that something is missing in their professional lives. Teaching is truly a rewarding profession. In addition to teachers, college students who may be reflecting on their own experiences or probing into the future looking for a career might find some inspiration in these pages. As an individual who has dedicated a life to my own education and those that would travel with me, I can posit that there is inherent nobility in the teaching profession. For those who are coming to terms with the realization that our society has an insatiable appetite for educated individuals, please keep reading. I want to encourage all of my readers, who may have been sidetracked, to return to college. There is no better way to fill oneself with enthusiasm than to participate in a community of individuals all looking to move their lives and their families' lives forward. Also, as a parent I want to share my perspectives on education and learning with other parents who may be thinking about their children's futures, especially in encouraging the pursuit and attainment of undergraduate and graduate degrees.

In these pages, I explore some of my own experiences as an administrator, teacher, and student. Rather than writing an academic discussion of Howard Gardner's Theory of Multiple Intelligences, this is my attempt to use the theory, like a pair of binoculars, to witness the sweep of experience, focus in on moments, and give some meaning to the story of my own life. Without spending too much time in technical jargon or magical mumbo jumbo, the book is an earnest attempt to tread water in the stormy currents between grounded real-world experience and the nebulous world of theory. It offers the reader ideas, memories, and a dream for the future. I offer you this book as a modest attempt to try to find a common wave which might gather a surge forward for all of us.

Zachary M. Oliver

"Intelligences are not things that can be seen or counted. Instead, they are potentials—presumably, neural ones—that will or will not be activated, depending upon the values of a particular culture, the opportunities available in that culture, and the personal decisions made by individuals and/or their families, schoolteachers, and others"

~ Howard Gardner

Multiple Intelligences Theory
A Forward

Finding myself working full-time as an instructor with a deeply troubled student body and freshly enrolled in a graduate program, I quickly began casting around trying to find my bearings. I worked through some great ideas quickly, such as Bloom's Taxonomy, which helped me to better organize my movement through information content for my students. This was great as I could see quickly that, for some of the population, this classically-ordered approach really showed immediate success in helping the students to grip the dynamics underlying the English language.

At the same time, I noticed that many of the other students still had trouble despite my new-found instructional savvy. At first, I thought that maybe the problem was them. Maybe the drugs they had probably taken before class or the anger problems that had incubated in them for a long time against formal education were clouding their senses. Then, a bit of wisdom took root.

Psychologists often say that if we don't elicit the response that we would like from other people, then we have to change our own behavior. So, I began to look at my own explanations. I started coming to terms with the realization that the students succeeding were those that I most easily engaged. In my mind, this meant that we had something in common. I thought maybe it was lifestyle or hobbies. I thought that maybe this commonality had to do with temperament. When I came across the Theory of Multiple Intelligences, I made another step in my self-analysis. I decided that all of my previous explanations might be correct as each goes a long way to talk about the way each of us engages the world. A powerful idea took shape.

I realized that those students who naturally engage the world most similarly to me had the easiest time accepting my explanations. They learned the best because they could "hear" me the best. It was then that my purpose as an instructor and my purpose as an educator deepened. From this point forward, I worked incessantly to create many multiple explanations for the same piece of knowledge that I felt was integral to my students' understanding of my subject, English grammar. This deep inspiration would not have been as readily accessible for me had I not been externally reinforced by the Theory of Multiple Intelligences.

Dr. Howard Gardner, the researcher on human intelligence who is credited with the Theory of Multiple Intelligences, is convinced that existing conceptions of intelligence are incomplete. Through his research on subjects suffering from brain injuries, he has participated in the demonstration that the brain has multiple abilities to process common information. Gardner tells the story of a brain that has many ways of handling multiple processes at any given time by applying parallel and complimentary centers to the challenge at hand.

The story is a beautiful one in that it does not try to relegate intelligence to any one part of the brain or method of processing information. Rather, it tells us of this amazing human capacity to creatively interact with the diversity of influence, experience, and environments of our world. In this story, human intelligence is a beautiful phenomenon that arises out of our will to contribute something that matters into the lives we lead.

Gardner has demonstrated that there are at least eight of these expressions, called "intelligences," that work together in order for us to provide some kind of skill that is important within the context of the cultures/communities to which we contribute our energy and effort.

While each of these intelligences assists us during everyday life, Gardner says that we tend to specialize in ways particular to our individual personality and the influence of our environments and communities. Even more peculiar and freeing, this theory also offers us the freedom to switch specializations through the changing needs of our culture and environment. The story that this theory tells us is that our intelligence, this great gift inside of each of us, is something far more flexible and free than it was once thought to be.

With a certain degree of excitement and trepidation, we all stand on a crossroad between a world that is becoming more and more anachronistic and a world which is quickly taking shape ahead of us. There is a powerful discussion across the social sciences concerning whether the tools that have held us together and focused for so long can continue to be stretched into this fantastically new future. This is an especially topical discussion for the future of education, which has already deeply invested in a new environment with new opportunities and constraints.

As with any research into human beings, the truths we discover always seem most rich as we look both into our own experience and then look for acknowledgement from the experience in the world. Once mandated by our memory, we look for resonance from the experts in our field, people who've also spent their life seeking milestones on the path to wisdom. At the intersection of book knowledge and life experience, we feel a caring voice welling up and filling us with a deeper energy, a reservoir which challenges us to also speak.

The interested reader may want to dig a bit deeper and try to work through an analysis of his or her own multiple intelligence analysis. For this person, I would suggest The Multiple Intelligences Developmental Assessment Scales test, or MIDAS, as an excellent starting place. Developed by Dr. Branton Shearer and approved by Dr. Howard Gardner, the MIDAS is not a test in the traditional sense of the word. It does not measure us against a scale that demonstrates intelligence, or lack thereof. The MIDAS identifies the intelligence matrix explained by the subject as he or she reveals his or her perceptions about everyday life. For more information concerning MIDAS and the Theory of Multiple Intelligence feel free to visit:

- http://www.miresearch.org
- http://www.infed.org/thinkers/gardner.htm
- http://tip.psychology.org/gardner.html

Zachary M. Oliver

"Bodily-Kinesthetic intelligence entails the potential of using one's whole body or part of the body (like the hand or the mouth) to solve problems or fashion products"

~ Howard Gardner

Chapter 1

Bodily-Kinesthetic Intelligence
Involving the Body

When we look at babies who are just beginning to recognize their tactile abilities, we can watch them quickly grab onto whatever is near. One of the first things that they discover is that there are these wonderful arms conveniently attached to their body that can be used to grasp this mysterious world.

It is mesmerizing to watch babies as they first become conscious of this ability. The child reaches out with big eyes trying to wiggle the fingers at the end of a chubby arm. These are not always smooth and carefully coordinated wiggles, though. The fingers sometimes open and close. Sometimes, the fingers refuse to cooperate. Each day, however, the movements become more and more connected, focused, and smooth. Soon, the infant wants to reach out and grasp with his or her hands this fascinating and complex world full of strange objects.

As a father deeply involved with the development of my children, I love to watch my daughters as they explore. I love to watch my youngest, who is only a couple of months old, as she reaches out with chubby fingers and begins to touch her world. While I know her world will be different than mine, I trust that it will be equally enthralling.

It is endearing, for example, if that thing that our child grabs is our finger. With arms stretched out, shoulders hunched, and a furrowed brow, our children describe the effort and concentration going on inside their mind and muscles. These are the kinds of moments that make parenthood a deeply satisfying and personal journey.

As a father, I have surely been humbled by my daughter, still only an infant, looking up at me with determination all over her face and eyes, as tiny fingers reach out to grab and squeeze my thumb. This gesture has been a special one for us, after all. It is one of the earliest active methods which allowed for us, father and baby, to bond. In fact, as her mother recovered after giving birth to her, I spent a few hours next to my daughter in the hospital nursery as she bathed in the heat from the warm lamps, touching her body and paying special attention to her hands and feet. She was making attempts even during those first hours out of the womb trying to grab my fingers as I accustomed her sense of touch.

Unfortunately, though, parenting isn't only filled with fond moments. It is, after all, frustrating if that thing our child grabs is our computer keyboard. A few magical letters might appear in that important email for our work supervisor which we left open and unattended on our desktop as we ran to the bathroom.

Of course, there is also the bizarre experience of watching our child open and close the refrigerator door repeatedly, even though it is absolutely clear that food is the last thing on their mind. While it is easy to get annoyed as we try to be parents and professionals, these are the funny little moments that characterize life for an infant. Sure, it is annoying, for example, for us to watch over and over as the refrigerator door opens and closes, sometimes smoothly, sometimes violently, as the child struggles to calibrate his or her muscles and balance to succeed in the act.

Although such small acts would seem insignificant to us adults, these are momentously exciting events in the lives of our children. I remember watching my older daughter practice her muscle control and dexterity with a screen door. She opened and closed that poor door for at least twenty minutes before I asked what she was doing. I don't remember her answer, but I do remember a beatific grin on her face that clearly expressed the transcendent joy of that moment of play.

Our child's search for dexterity may even become painful if, for example, in the process of exploring the world with their hands, he or she decides to honk our nose. I'll never forget those winces of pain I see on my wife's face as our infant daughter's hands ball up with a firm grip on her hair. Our youngest daughter always looks over at me with a shiny face that communicates wonder and happiness even though my wife's feelings, bless her, are far from such a happy and innocent place.

It's a true challenge. Parents of toddlers spend much of their time running around just behind their children, as soon as the child can walk, and struggle to keep them from exploring electric outlets, oven tops, and garbage cans with their little fingers. Parents do this because they know more about what purpose, positive and negative, each of these modern tools offer to us than infants, who engage these dangerous products with one of our most efficient and quickly developed sense tools, the fingers.

Every parent gets excited when witnessing the progress of a child. While I am no great expert in developmental psychology, I think this is because, on some level, we recognize that this exploration of the environment with our sense of touch is the display of some kind of intelligence. Gardner calls this "kinesthetic" and talks about it at length as a much-misunderstood expression of intelligence among older children and developing adults. We recognize the intelligence of a toddler's exploration, but not as much with an adolescent. The world of an older child is designed with a much different aesthetic. After early elementary school, after all, the child's environment is characterized by whiteboards, PowerPoint presentations and fill-in-the-blank handouts. For highly kinesthetic children, this shift must generate a world view that must make them feel negative towards their natural learning style.

When we recognize people who can use their hands to create beautiful and interesting things, we usually call these people "talented" or "deft," but not necessarily intelligent. In fact, more often than not, we may think of these people as strange or peculiar, depending on their social skills.

This bias is carried by the students with a strong primary kinesthetic preference, who will commonly be addressed with negative attention from teachers due to their inability to focus and succeed on traditional tests. Furthermore, these students often get the message that they are stupid due to their frustration and failure on tests which are designed in such a manner that all of their weaknesses emerge simultaneously when the teacher addresses the class by saying "All right, class, I hope everyone is ready for the test. Put away your books. Take out a piece of paper. Keep your eyes on your own paper at all times".

Refusing to take our share of the responsibility, we say that students are less prepared than ever, the students are not as intelligent as they used to be, and that all of these non-academic courses are weakening the students' abilities to develop intellectual and analytical skills. The poor performance, though, is indicative of a gap between our methods of teaching and the complex learning needs of our students.

A quick scan of the average classroom reveals a whole collection of what we, as forceful instructors with our expectations, consider to be defiant behaviors. With a wink and a nod, Gardner and I would agree that what's really happening in these situations is that a disengaged mental state is being communicated by the students through their powerful non-verbal body gestures. Some of these students may be so traumatized from year after year of failure that this disengagement may even be a carefully studied and deeply invested-in perception of self.

Consider the setting of a typical high school: In a typical classroom with rows of desks that neatly face the chalk board or white board at the front of the class, everyone, in the ideal version, sits quietly attentive and scribbling notes as the teacher lectures. The teacher writes a few key points on the board or, if he or she is technologically savvy, on a presentation beamed onto a screen from a sleek laptop computer.

The teacher, in this setting, commands attention. If anyone talks, then there are repercussions. Detention lingers over all of the students' heads. So, there are only a couple of ways this moment can play out. The students either play-along and focus as successfully as possible, space out and bide time until recess or shop class, or act out and escape because of detention, suspension, and even dismissal.

This story probably hits closer to home as we remember that teenager which continues to live on deep inside of us, despite years of adult pressure and maturity. While some of us quietly sat in these oppressive classroom environments and daydreamed about freedom, others among us took advantage of a teacher's turned back to pass notes, and some of us simply fidgeted uncomfortably, trying to find something to do with our hands in order to keep our minds occupied.

Some of these were the guys and girls who were often masters at athletics and lived for recess, lunch, and P.E. In an articulate expression of intelligence, they kept all of the rules and strategies in mind while running up and down the basketball courts and football fields that feature so prominently in our high school consciousness. Some of us feel most alive while playing sports. We each have a complex inter-relation between our linked minds and bodies. After all, our minds, regardless of how intelligent we are, cannot engage a body which is unprepared, un-muscled, and uncoordinated. In much the same way, a strong body cannot continue to stay strong if it cannot engage a mind that is not focused.

Despite all of the busyness of our lives, my wife and I have spent many hours during our years in graduate school taking long walks while exploring many of the complex ideas hidden within challenging textbooks. This habit has continued for us. We now walk a couple of times a week and spend the time discussing issues at work and dream of creative solutions to elegantly handle these challenges. In fact, the methodology used for my doctoral dissertation was first developed during one of these walks and went through considerable revision throughout many weeks as my wife and I circled around Diamond Head and watched the setting sun.

Returning to our long-faded memories of high school, we vaguely remember the guys and girls who would sleep through geometry class and flunk every test, but would walk into shop class and create fantastic structures featuring challenging tolerances measured in decimals moving out to the thousandths place or challenging cakes decorated with mind-boggling attention to detail in Home Economics class. These were the friends and colleagues of ours who were completely uninterested in English or History class, but who would come alive at the thought of working on a project that somehow allowed them to get their hands on materials that could be molded and shaped into something interesting, beautiful, and sometimes even delicious.

Not all of these students invested in a high degree of specialization in kinesthetic intelligence were able to get through those boring classes with nothing more than a pencil to keep their hands busy. Many of them were the guys and girls who would ditch school day after day and end up getting kicked out due to non-compliance with school policy. It didn't matter to them, though. They were only happy when covered in the grease and soot of a tired old motor that offered up to them endless lessons into the secrets of internal combustion.

A few of my friends went this way. Instead of cars, though, they became deeply and passionately involved in the creation of surfboards. The curves and angles of a surfboard fascinated them. They could obsess for hours over fractions of an inch here and there as they sanded the foam blank preparing it for its fiberglass shell. They would literally spend hours making sure that the edges of the surfboard, called rails, were shaped as closely to perfection, in their minds, as possible.

For me, I was only interested if the board, once it was in the water, was functional. The kinesthetic intelligence was not my most evolved one. I preferred making my craft the art of riding the wave, not of shaping the board. I did dabble, however, into the highly kinesthetic craft of wood-working and apprenticed myself as a harp builder. I learned many interesting things about wood and finishes while developing my skills at shaping and finishing these beautiful Koa and Redwood Kinnors. The most interesting thing I learned about myself was that I much prefer to play instruments than to make them.

As a musician, I spend my time often in a daze. I find my fingers wanting to touch an instrument. My mind listens to the noise of everyday life and craves to find order in it. In college, I used to haunt the record stores on Telegraph Street in Berkeley looking for exotic new sounds. Sometimes, I would find great walls of guitar feedback. Or, I might discover a perfect moment inside of the clanging and mechanical claustrophobic racket of an industrial rhythm. Perhaps, in a different mood, the rebelliousness and shamanism of reggae or the otherworldly and timeless drones of an Indian raga might reach out from the speaker and fill my ears with inspiration.

With that inspiration, I sat for hours and worked my fingers through scales and chords looking for a way to make my ears hear a new song and to share that song with anyone who might listen. I entertained thoughts of pursuing music as a career. I almost declared music as my major. My family encouraged me to accept an alternative. They pointed out my enduring love of books as a much more reasonable pursuit.

So, I spent the next few years deeply involved with all kinds of stories and ideas. From Frankenstein to Faulkner and Plato to Pynchon, I was exposed to the classics. I took every opportunity to go off the beaten track, however. I loved the oral traditions of the Native Americans represented by writers such as Sherman Alexie, Leslie Marmon Silko, and Louis Erdrich. Maxine Hong Kingston and Ishmael Reed featured as guest speakers for those of us willing to peer just past the obvious at what storytelling might become. I lapped it all up and craved a time when I might adventure, a time when I might begin absorbing my own story. Little did I know that I was already deep in the process of soaking up a wonderful life. Lennon really had it when he said that "life is what happens while you're busy making plans."

Upon graduating college, I was told, as so many of us are, that I was trained to be a leader of the next generation. I was told that a Bachelor of English degree with a specialty in Multicultural and Anglophone Studies from U.C. Berkeley would generate success. I was told a very convoluted truth that couldn't begin to describe the circuitous journey that I would have to venture along before finding anything resembling success. After 3 years and 2 bouts of unemployment, I ended up working in a dead-end retail job selling pillows and massagers.

Employers didn't care that I could recite Heinrich Heine or that I enjoyed the writing of Ngũgĩ Wa Thiong'o. They just wanted someone who could close a sale. All I wanted to do was find something to which I could contribute, but pillows and massagers didn't really seem to be the noble future which could fulfill me. It was at this point that I began casting about looking at a chance to apply my degree. I could either write and be broke or teach. Teaching was something that I had projected into my future, but not this quickly, not in my early twenties.

The early twenties are a precarious time of life. Reflecting on my own experience, I felt lost. I had worked through a challenging degree, but couldn't find any employment to match. I was knowledgeable enough to know that I had entered some kind of post-university purgatory: one that affected me with a malaise that spread throughout my reality. I wandered from job to job. I had moved from apartment to apartment trading roommates and lease agreements along the way. At this point, though, I had failed all the way to my parent's house and had to make my bed, literally and figuratively, in the dining room under the table.

Thinking that their son was going to be a success after completing a university degree, my parents had wisely downsized their living quarters to a one bedroom. While they understood the challenges of finding a career path to a degree and graciously shared whatever space they had, I'm sure they worried about what kind of dark cloud had stretched across my bright future. I certainly didn't want to be "that guy" that lived with his mom and dad leeching off of them for a place to live and eat while indulging in some kind of weird Peter Pan fantasy.

Even then, stumbling around in a post-college hangover, there was a question inside me looking for a solid answer. Who should I be? What place does this world have to offer me? How do I find this place, this person? In an act of desperation, I answered an advertisement to teach English in South Korea.

In this advertisement, a meeting was announced that would take place at 11:00AM at a golf course clubhouse. While I thought that this was an odd place to show up for a job interview, I figured that an open mind would probably set the tone for what might be a fascinating adventure. Strolling right off the green with a putter still in his hand, the Korean businessman, with the ubiquitous moniker "Mr. Kim," took one look at me and asked in a thick accent to prove that I was a college graduate. Luckily, I had brought my diploma.

After checking to see if I had a passport, he told me that I would fly to Korea on Saturday. It was Thursday. I thought he was joking. He told me that a secretary would contact my home with instructions for where I would pick up my flight coupon, spun on his heels, and exited. Before I even consciously became aware that I had just agreed to go to Korea for a year to work for a man whom I met at a golf course in Honolulu, he was gone. Mr. Kim never even shook my hand at the end of this interview. He merely turned around, walked back out onto the golf course, and stepped back into his little cart. He quickly accelerated down the path and out of sight. Reeling, I began to think that I had just been scammed.

I drove away from this meeting sure that this had been another case of some "big talker" having a little fun at my expense. I didn't believe for a second that any secretary would make any attempt to reach me and that a ticket would be forthcoming. All of this seemed like a dream.

When I returned home, there was a message from a secretary, though. She directed me to a nearby travel agent and said that a ticket for a Saturday morning flight was waiting for me. Without another word, I packed my bags, said goodbye to my cozy hideout under the dining-room table, and watched one last January sunset in Hawaii, knowing that the bitter cold of a Korean winter was waiting for me.

Nothing, not all of the stories about blue fingers and toes among veterans of the Korean conflict, could have prepared me for the absolute misery that awaited me upon my arrival at Kimpo Airport at the end of January 1999.

Another Mr. Kim, this one shorter and less well-dressed than the first, picked us up from the airport and drove us to the small provincial capital city, Suwon, which is about an hour from Seoul. With nary a word in English, he drove me and another recently-arrived malcontent expatriate who would be my roommate for the next year to our apartment, handed us the keys, pointed us in the direction of the taxi stand, and told us with halting English to wait for another Mi-Guk foreign teacher in the morning. No specific time was mentioned. No specific place was indicated. The stage was set for the next day, my first day of teaching: the first day of my new career.

Needless to say, my grumpy roommate and I were wandering around by about 4 AM. Besides the jetlag that was beating our wounded psyches across the dateline, we were deathly afraid of missing our meeting with the half-expected Mi-Guk English teacher. As we shivered in a doorway trying to escape the dreadfully cold pre-dawn Yellow Wind sweeping down the Korean peninsula from Siberian China looming to the North, we wondered what kind of madness had gotten into us to choose this contract to come to a country that was still very much off the beaten path.

By the time the sun came up, we were so cold that we had actually run out of things to say. I think that our souls were trying to come to grip with the absolute misery of the moment. We finally saw a foreign face and stumbled out into the cold to ask if he was our contact. He took one look at us and showed us to a taxi. We were blissfully unaware of just what awaited us inside of the Korean taxi.

Nothing can prepare the relatively tame Western car experience with a Korean taxi. It may be that it pales in comparison to the insanity that is the taxi ride in the Philippines or Bangladesh, but for us, at that moment, heart-stopping doesn't even begin to express the feeling of terror we experienced. As we were tossed from side to side slamming into the taxi's doors, hoping for the door locks to be solid, watching bumpers and pedestrians slide within inches of our rickety little car that pumped the crazy-fast Korean Bong Chak beat at full volume, punctuated with what could only be Korean curse words made up of vowels and consonant groups around which none of us could even imagine wrapping our tongues.

I can't remember exactly, but I think I actually fell onto the nasty pavement as I exited this little terror ride. A moment after picking myself off the sidewalk, I was assaulted with myriad sensations: pickled cabbage called Kim Chee, fish, urine, cigarettes, diesel fumes, and the indelible rhythm of vomit pulsing just underneath.

I have always been a gastric adventurer. I've always been one to pop something into my mouth before asking what it is and how it's prepared, but this first morning in Korea had me second-guessing my entire reality. One of the Korean teachers saw how bitter cold I must have looked and put something warm into my hands. I thanked her and ate half before realizing that she had presented to me a cup full of silk-worm larvae: a Korean snack for cold mornings called Bon De Gee, not to be confused with Korean popcorn called Bong Ti Gee.

After this cultural assault, an ambulance screeched to a halt in front of us, the doors flew open, and two uniformed individuals jumped out, saluted us, and proceeded to manhandle us into the back. It only took one look from the fellows to communicate that I better find something on which to find traction, something to hang onto, lest I fly around the back of the ambulance and find myself, ironically, needing medical attention.

With sirens blaring, the breakneck pace of the morning resumed with us alternately getting slammed against the rear doors as the ambulance accelerated and then slammed against the front wall as the drivers braked for pedestrians who seemed oblivious that the ambulance brakes could fail and squash them. The end of the drive was punctuated with the doors being thrown open and two M16 A1 rifles being lifted from the firing position before some smart salutes were snapped in our direction.

It turned out that my first class was going to be at the South Korean Police Officers Training Institute. Mr. Kim, the shorter, less well-dressed version, handed me a book, pointed me to a room, and said something that sounded like: "Three-hour class, then lunch." After he walked away, I looked at the other teachers and verified if my ears had actually heard what I thought.

Like a punch to the gut, I found that it was true. I had neither taught a thing, nor had I ever studied anything about education. Being the baby in the family, I hadn't even gotten any practice on little brothers and sisters. I had nothing but a little English book with the prerequisite grammar exercises peppered with some cheesy and unrealistic cartoons designed to generate a simple conversation, and my less than stellar personality complete with jetlag and sticky car-sickness.

There was a moment and a choice. I had to decide whether I was going to go into the room acting as some kind of mechanized expert and deliver a book which I had never seen to a class that I didn't know, or whether I was going to walk into the room as a flawed human being bent on understanding a group of people who were born on the far side of the world, who were raised on a radically different cultural aesthetic than my own, and who were probably not much more motivated than I was at the prospect of a three-hour class.

Perhaps I was just immature, an untrained and unprepared teacher. Maybe, I was reacting to the craziness and stress of having just jumped into a new life in a new environment that was much further from anything I could expect. Maybe I was, because of my lack of formal training, looking at the situation with a beginner's eye. While I was ready to participate in the moment and soak up this wild new life, I was far from ready to wear a staid professional identity. I was still, after all, on a journey to find my own self.

As I look back, I see myself as a baby, just beginning to reach out, brow furrowed in determination, trying to find a way to grasp a strange new world.

Whatever the reason, I walked into the anonymous sea of uniformed police cadets as a human being and spent the first three hours merely trying to get my ears to hear and my tongue to pronounce the 30 exotic names of which not one sounded familiar. These rare and beautiful names included: Eu Chun, Ji Tae, Bong Gu, Mi Yong, and Yun Sun, just to name a few.

It seemed self-evident to me that we, as students and teachers, must reciprocate a fundamental respect for one another that begins as we try to learn names and become familiar with each other. Clumsy as it was, my attempt to learn the students' names was a very real and physical way to show respect for these people in whose world I had just appeared.

Suffice to say that my world, my identity, and my career direction was shaped and will continue to be shaped by those first three hours, the following three-hour class after lunch, and the three-hour class after dinner on my first whole day spent in Korea. My learning, that day, was visceral and very hands-on.

All of my preconceptions about teaching, I realized in that moment, were couched in my reality as a student. Up there, in front of the class, I was no longer a student. It was time to reassess and begin to find some ways to be aware of my role as a mentor, as someone who might assist people to become better, but not to dictate what that improvement is.

***

I didn't know it at the time, but one of the wonderful aspects about the Theory of Multiple Intelligences is that Gardner specifically states, over and over, that no one intelligence is more important than any other and that, furthermore, every single one of us carries each of these intelligences within us, even if we've chosen not to specialize with it.

Many years later, upon my discovery of Gardner, I began thinking about how the kinesthetic experience could play out in an English class. At first, I was shy about it and didn't know where to start. Inspired by my memory of the first day in Korea, I started small.

On the first day of class, each quarter, I would work around the classroom and memorize everyone's name. This always surprised everyone. The students weren't used to being noticed. At the same time, I felt that this challenge that I issued myself was very serious. The students always asked how I remembered their names. The secret is simple: I used brute force. I forced myself to call each of them over and over on the first couple of days until their names became comfortable in my mouth. This was an excellent start and helped me to grow as a teacher by identifying new techniques that helped me to physically engage the students in my class.

New challenges awaited me. Before class, I liked to stand in the hallway, hold the door open, and shake each person's hand. This wasn't done only in the spirit of custom, even though it did set a tone for the class. Mostly, I wanted each student to know that we were connected in a respectful way. Before long, I noticed that students, even when they came in late or saw me at the movie theater on the weekend, would always go out of their way to shake my hand to let me know that we were connected by some common experience.

The idea of much of our education system is based on the idea that education builds community. While I realize that touch is often culture specific in its norms, I would venture a guess that all community begins through some kind of formalized touch. The connection that I initiated in my class through the development of our culture created the basis for a community built on a trust that everyone felt and which began with touch.

"Interpersonal intelligence denotes a person's capacity to understand the intentions, motivations, and desires of other people and, consequently, to work effectively with others"

~ Howard Gardner

Chapter 2

Interpersonal Intelligence
Working with Others

My memory of middle school often conjures up fond memories of lunch breaks and recess. This, in some sense, seems odd. I can't help but judge that it is somehow wrong that my memories of middle school are framed by the especially vivid moments in between classes instead of all of the great instructional moments that occurred during those long hours of class time. After all, it raises the question: Why would anyone go to school if, later in life, the only solid memory of it is actually during the spaces of time in between classes and not the classes themselves?

The dizzyingly fast tetherball twists and the playful but sometimes violent games of dodge ball are all clearer memories for me than who were my fifth through eighth grade teachers, or what was taught in Math, Science, or Health.

I have no doubt that I've learned the material from those classes. At the same time, I have to be frank and honest with myself and recognize that the memories were vacuumed up during my first two years of college, and by watching Discovery, National Geographic, and the History Channel as an adult, or through interesting discussions with my well-informed friends studying for degrees in these functional areas.

In the case of Mathematics: The ubiquitous order of operations, sometimes called PEMDAS, didn't find a place in my conscious mind until I audited a basic math class while working at the college as an English instructor. Instead of being attentive during class, my days during late elementary through middle school were filled with focus on social interactions.

Playing on soccer teams, baseball teams, and making friends at the beach are bright spots in my developmental milestones. I think that this reality speaks to a larger challenge: Our education system has developed in a manner divergent with our natural predilections; specifically, my memory of the spaces in between classes characterizes the mismatch that exists between what educators think we should be and what we actually are in the experience of young people reaching towards maturity.

Recess was when we really came alive. While sitting in the classrooms with single lines of nondescript desks all facing forward, some of us were probably a bit like mental zombies seeking correct answers instead of live brains. And like zombies, we were slow in our pursuit of the correct answer. Our minds were still young, of course. We were certainly only somewhere at the beginning of a long developmental curve. We desperately wanted to please the teacher. It's almost as if we were programmed to go into a trance and simply grasp for whatever answers the teacher led us toward in a thoughtless pursuit of task completion.

Unfortunately, there was no strategy in our pursuit. So, we often called out answers that were, while imaginative, incorrect. It's easy to laugh about this now, but this sad reality tells the observant researcher that we, as young students, were building what is known in teacher-speak as incorrect schema. This means that we were, in our rush to produce correct answers, building weak foundations on which later learning would rely. My lack of understanding concerning PEMDAS is a perfect example.

My poor schema for mathematics has plagued me for many years. I have, for my whole adult life, felt limited because of an insecurity that I have concerning my performance in Mathematics. More than anything else, I can track my failure to pursue an early dream of a career as an astronaut to this weakness in manipulating numbers.

Perhaps we were mindless in this pursuit because the right answer earned us gold stars, the teacher's praise, or a pat on the back. We thought that the right answer would make us "right" as individuals, like a proof of future success or something. Nothing of the sort is the case, however. We were often told how important it was to perform in school as our futures would rely on our success or failure. Our prepubescent noses were rubbed in this not so self-evident truth.

When questioned about it, the adults pointed out that research says that students who do well in early educational experience will perform at much higher levels later in life. Here's a dirty little secret, though: There is an old research adage that states that correlation does not necessarily indicate causation. This means that just because two things happen at the same time and in the same way, it doesn't mean that they are connected. Success in later life may have nothing to do with intense effort during our secondary education.

So, back in our middle school classrooms, when we did attain the right answer, nothing magical happened. Sure, maybe we earned the "A" or the gold star. Maybe, because the class did well, we earned a popcorn party on Friday, but nothing really fundamentally changed for us. It's not as if the stars aligned and our future as a chief justice of the Supreme Court, a world-renowned theoretical physicist, or god-like and famous brain surgeon became palpable.

Because of our focus on being correct or earning the points or gold stars, our brains and body didn't ooze with pleasure or satisfaction from the learning. We traded the ineffable pleasure of learning for something palpable in our focus. Don't think for a second that I'm saying that it's a shame that we don't feel pleased by learning. We probably always will feel pleased by our growth; we just, in our rush for the A or the gold star, don't focus on it. Also, the early experiences of learning don't give us much of a rush. There was simply too much trauma involved. I just wasn't capable of understanding that this kind of experience, an appreciation for learning, existed until I reached the end of high school. And even then, I didn't experience the joy that comes from learning as a deeply personal experience until much later in life, after I returned to graduate school.

Sitting at my computer late at night pounding out paper after paper on my battered computer keyboard or while sitting in a room with a bunch of intelligent peers discussing the vagaries of leadership or research methodology, I sometimes felt as if I was having peek experiences, like Mozart at a harpsichord or Einstein having a breakthrough at some Princeton chalkboard. In contrast, those early years brought, the few times I was able to present the correct answer, nothing more than a frail or hollow sense of success.

Maybe the lack of joy was because we, in our teenage minds, thought we, as a species, already knew everything. During those long forgotten days of secondary school, we simply continued the pursuit of the next right answer. Question after answer, rinse, and repeat; there was little to no cognitive development or development of consciousness. The ideas and concepts never needed to be integrated, unless they related directly to answers A, B, C, or all of the above.

There is, after all, not much of an opportunity to find oneself in a world in which we are forced to do nothing but follow directions and prove things that our teachers already know. It certainly doesn't seem like a very motivating environment.

What those long middle years of school felt like, as I remember, was waiting. It was like we were all sitting there in class waiting for the rest of our life to happen, like a metaphysical waiting room. And on those days, as soon as the bell rang, the world would spring into action. We pictured ourselves jumping up from our desks and running outside screaming with each tick of the second hand on the big clock hanging just over the door to the classroom-prison. It's almost as if each hour in class coiled the spring tighter and tighter for those few minutes we could run, play, and most of all socialize. We spent much of our time memorizing who liked whom, who was having conflict with whom, and who was best and worst at whatever the most important skill was at that point, whether that skill was jump ropes or basketball.

The point is that we are social creatures. Even those among us who would like to deny the need or cultivate an image apart from society still need contact, a relationship that helps us to define the ideas that zip around our brains.

Once a relationship is established, we derive a lot of joy from it. Maybe this isn't a joy in the traditional sense, complete with smiles and laughs. It might be a joy that is perverse, something that the psychological community might define as maladaptive.

However this joy might be described, it is a defining experience for us as we move along in our development. Most importantly, it is a joy that cannot be experienced alone. When I consider my own defining relationships, I can see a whole gamut of lessons that teach me about what I've been and who I might become.

Looking back at that first week in South Korea, I only remember flashes of myself stumbling from school to classroom to taxi to bed and then waking before the first light of day to repeat the process. I remember walking, for the first time, down the bustling side streets and seeing stores, bars, and restaurants climbing the buildings. Instead of shops on the first floor, here, in Suwon, the buildings were packed vertically with every kind of pleasure one can imagine: billiards, hairstylists, hostess bars. These are just a few meager examples that leap to mind. Thousands of blinking neon signs and blaring K-pop music pumped through the lingering fumes of stale alcohol and cigarettes.

I can still glimpse the throngs of people hand in hand, boys with boys and girls with girls, all giggling and wearing pointy shoes with curled-up toes, eating wild cherry ice cream from Baskin Robbins during one of those late January afternoons. I remember that I couldn't get the heat turned on in my apartment and therefore had to take cold showers until I got so sick that a new Korean friend felt sorry for me, followed me home, and taught me how to turn it on and off, but not how to change the temperature. For the next few weeks, I had to battle between being too hot or too cold. The control panel for the heating system was in Korean, as it should be in Korea, and I had no idea how to read it.

I remember the potent medicine that was dispensed in the Korean pharmacies in pouches which mixed powerful western-style drugs with Chinese herbs. After taking it, I saw stars and felt better almost immediately. I remember coming home in the evening after a long day of teaching and maneuvering in my new culture, looking at my wild eyes in the mirror, and washing my face. As the cold water ran over me, I could see this yellow-gray silt dripping off of me. It was, for lack of a more sophisticated term, pollution. Up to this point in my life, pollution was an abstraction. Pollution was something to be discussed in school or around an earnest group of coffee-drinking college friends. It wasn't supposed to be real, not like this, not running off my face like makeup. I understood, at the time, that this was a price of success for Korea's developing status in the world. This was a way for Korea to emerge onto the world stage as an economic powerhouse. I had never experienced a world so bent on industrial success. I had no idea at the time how completely involved in this world I would become.

On my first Friday evening just after class, I emerged right behind the students to find Mr. Kim, the well-dressed and tall version, waiting for me. This was our first meeting since our whirlwind interview at a Honolulu golf club just a week before. In his typical, all-business fashion, he asked me to come to work for a half day on Saturday. He asked me to dress well and to meet him at the taxi stand close to the apartment in the morning. I had no idea what to expect, but I did as I was bid. Mr. Kim only "asked" because he knew that this was an American mannerism. I never, for a second, had a choice in the matter. Despite not having much experience in Korea at that point, it was clear to me that power in this world was valued and wielded without subtlety or fanfare.

In the morning, I jumped into Mr. Kim's car along with a couple of other teachers and quickly sped down a pot-hole filled one-lane road that led us within minutes out of the city and into terraced rice paddies that engulfed a hilly rural area. The difference between the city with its hustle and noise and this was stark.

There was no gradual divide between the urban and the rural. A crumbling wall topped with some old Kee-Wa masonry represented the border between the two. This old wall was like a time machine transporting the bouncing car back a hundred years or more to a time before Kim Jung Il's radical Juche ideology, and the DMZ splitting North and South Korea that still sends shivers up tourists' spines, or the Japanese occupation that ushered Korea into the modern era.

Bumping along this small road, we came around a hill and were surprised to discover a giant, red, polished granite office compound ahead. There were uniformed guards outside standing at attention. Waving us into a stream of cars, the security guards aimed Mr. Kim for the parking lot. After parking our car, we walked into the security building and were asked to sit in a waiting room that was not unlike an airport. Inside this room were at least 25 other teachers each looking a bit disoriented, but trying to put on an air of self-control. Their darting eyes and restless hands gave them away. I don't blame them; a quick glance out the window revealed that the guards were fully armed with automatic submachine guns and belts that clearly carried hand grenades.

This was hardly the sophisticated urban Asian world that calls out to an American ex-patriot English teacher as an adventure of a lifetime.

A well-dressed young lady moved efficiently through the teachers with a clipboard. She had a security guard with her. As she made eye contact with me, I noticed that her clipboard had a picture of me and a resume. Up until this moment, I really had no idea what was going on, but the request for fine clothes, the room full of ex-patriot teachers, and the resume with picture spelled out that this was some kind of bizarre job interview. Yet, the clipboard-carrying young lady never asked me anything. She simply shook my hand, looked me in the eye, and thanked me in Korean for, as I later found out, coming to the Samsung Semiconductor compound. After finally piling back into the car and retracing our way to Suwon City, Mr. Kim seemed happy and decided to treat us to his favorite lunch: Burger King.

It was great fun for Mr. Kim to watch us order for ourselves at the counter. The Whopper, when said in a Korean-English—Konglish—accent, sounds like "Hwa Pa." The Korean staff and Mr. Kim took great pains not to snicker too badly as we struggled over and over to order our lunch with our perfect American accents. We were all hungry, though, and put up with the ribbing pretty well. I remember feeling how odd it was that we, as Americans, were mispronouncing our own words to the Burger King employees.

At the end of our lunch, Mr. Kim asked me to stay behind for a moment to speak with him. He told me that I had been given a great honor. He explained that the President of Samsung Semiconductor, Mr. Sun, had selected me to serve as his English teacher. He added that I needed to treat this contract with the seriousness that it deserved. He told me that I should work strictly from the book and not to deviate from the curriculum as it was set out in the prescribed book. Finally, he explained that I needed to be at the taxi stand at 6 AM on Monday where I would be met and taken for my first introduction.

Excited, I was out at the taxi stand at 5:30. I did not want to miss this. I had no idea what to expect, but I knew that this morning would be important; perhaps, it would be the most important one of my life up to that point. Silently, this sleek white car pulled up to where I stood, a uniformed man jumped out and swung the door open for me, and I sank into the luxurious seat of a Samsung sedan. This executive car somehow managed to float above the potholes scattered on the single-lane country road as we raced the rising sun straight to the Samsung compound.

This time, as we approached the Samsung compound, the security guards opened the gate, flashed a stiff salute, and quickly unblocked the path as we slipped through. Before I knew what was happening, a door opened and I moved through it. I was following another attractive young administrative assistant up an elevator and down a hallway where I was ushered into a giant darkened conference room decorated with beautiful wood and ultra modern paintings. I was left there in the dark for a few minutes wondering how this phenomenal room found its way to this remote corner of South Korea nestled amongst hills in the middle of terraced rice paddies.

I remember that I was dozing when the door swung open flooding the room with light. I saw a man bow low in silhouette before the smartly-dressed young lady from the interview and a very tall 50-something year old distinguished-looking bald man entered the room. He stood there in the light with a double breasted pin-striped suit and a small sad smile punctuated with powerful eyes that snuck out from under heavy lids. He said a few words in Korean to the lady while smiling at me. The lady looked at me, nodded to him, and backed out of the room closing the doors behind her while bowing almost completely to the ground.

The man, the president of the second largest computer chip producing company in the world, straightened his suit jacket, moved forward, and extended his hand to me. He introduced himself using his first name in a completely unassuming manner.

Using his first name in such a casual and friendly manner struck me as an odd gesture as everyone around him was deeply deferential whenever he said anything to them. While I will call him Mr. Sun due to the deep respect that I have for this man, he taught me a valuable lesson in our first interaction on that morning. With a simple act, he wiped away the space that hierarchies can make between individuals. With the familiarity bred by the sound of a first name, Mr. Sun opened the pathways of communication between us: not teacher and student, but co-adventurer and incessant co-questioner.

For the next year, I spent almost every morning sipping tea, watching the sun rise, and discussing the great mysteries and monuments of our human species with this great man. We started by reading magazine articles together and discussing the politics, culture, and intrigue that coursed through the words. We kept returning to the importance of aesthetics as a tool which informs our journey through life. The English pedagogy book that Mr. Kim had admonished me to stick with seemed like a superficial path in the face of our philosophical investigations. Besides, Mr. Sun's English was impeccable, as was his Japanese and German.

It quickly became apparent to me that my success as a teacher with Mr. Sun would not be in my great command of the English language, but in my interest in the radically different world which formed Mr. Sun. I approached each morning as a student, not as a teacher. I listened to him discuss with me the vagaries of semiconductor manufacturing, the intense scrutiny of Samsung in an economy that had just received IMF aid, and the twisted realities of South and North Korean politics and the complex and ancient historical contexts on which these countries have been developed.

My ongoing success as an educator is directly related to the realization that I was not there to tell Mr. Sun, or any of my other students, what to think. Instead, I was, and continue to be, present in the learning moment as another student, another member of the community, representing a radically different perspective, no better —no worse. Learning happened in this arena with this compatriot because neither of us, Mr. Sun nor I, insisted in forming some artificial dynamics that became stifled with strict adherence to some kind of tired role. Instead, we designed our meetings as an inspiration for cognition.

This spirit is something that I've only recognized in hindsight. It was easy to create this kind of energy in a one-on-one intimate setting, such as the kind which I shared with Mr. Sun. In the college setting, I didn't "get" this right away. Years went by as I struggled to find a way to introduce this spirit that I had enjoyed with Mr. Sun with my regular student population in classes with sometimes as many as thirty students. This is the thing about maturity: it doesn't happen all at once. More than anything, it seems that we will look back at the sweeping arc of our life and look for evidence of who we are in our actions and interactions with others as evidence of our maturity at any given moment of our life.

When I was about four years old, I was surprised with a beautiful dog, an afghan hound. He was a gangly little puppy with a love for shoes. I remember that, in those early years, we had to hide our shoes just out of reach of his powerful jaws. Despite being somewhat irreverent, my family named him in homage of his ancestry. He was called "Sufi." This dog was my companion in my early years. I remember coming home from school and watching

Sufi excitedly run around the yard and come crashing into me.

During summer vacation, as I got older, I received a chore that I didn't much like because of Sufi. Besides picking up his poop, I had to scrub the nice white walls outside of our family's home that Sufi so loved to rub. His long and shaggy coat would leave greasy dirt lines along the sides of our walkway. In my immaturity, this frustrated me. This clearly set the stage for a behavior that I'm eternally ashamed of, but one which defines a capacity which I need to stay aware of in order to ensure that this is not repeated in my adult life as a family man.

Once, during one of the last days of school when almost everyone, including the teacher, was looking at the clock hoping to watch it spin its way to 2:30 and the bright sun reminded us of the beautiful beach, I was dreading the end of the day. I was having a rough time at school. I don't know exactly why, but Jeff and Eric, my two best friends, were acting weird. On that day, they wouldn't talk to me, include me in their plans, or meet me to ride bikes home from school. At recess and at lunch, I was the object of jeers and mean-spirited insults. We typically all met at the end of the school day and rode our bikes down the hill together before splitting directions on our way home. But this time the two of them had ditched me just as the bell rang.

Because I was slow leaving the class, I had been unable to get out to the bike rack quickly. By the time I raced over there, they were gone. My bike was knocked over in their rush to ditch me.

So, I fought back my shame, unlocked my bike, climbed on and started pedaling down the driveway and out to the hill. As I rounded the corner outside the school, something smacked my helmet, disintegrated, and showered dirt into my eyes. I looked around and saw Jeff, with a mischievous look on his face, following through on a hard overhand throw just as a big dirt clod exploded against my shoulder. Eric was there, as well, having just ducked behind the mailbox after delivering the first head shot. Their bikes were parked in such a way that I couldn't have noticed them as I came down the driveway. This was an ambush, pure and simple, designed to tell me that I was no longer welcome in that social circle. I didn't know what I had done or why I was being ostracized, but I'm sure that the tears fell hard as I pedaled as fast as possible to get home and away from them.

And there was Sufi in the garden as I came up the steps. He had a bone and looked to be enjoying it. This must have been a special occasion for him as we never gave him bones. He looked up at me for a second, but he was really much more interested in gnawing that juicy treat that still had meat hanging from it. He was focused on sucking every last bit of juice from it as possible. I walked past him into the house where I was greeted by a note that directed me to the garden. On that day, I was supposed to pick up Sufi's messes and to begin scrubbing the white walls of Sufi's dirt trail.

Besides the simple fact that picking up Sufi's dog poop was my least favorite chore, scrubbing the wall was probably one of the hardest and most time consuming. On this day, fresh from the beating my so-called friends had given me, I was well beyond my reservoirs of grace.

I dragged myself out to the yard and shoveled a few of Sufi's sloppy sliders into the garbage. The heat got to me quickly, though. I don't remember if this was a heat that came from the sun or if this was a heat that was building inside of me as I flashed back to the look on Jeff's face as the dirt clod whizzed towards me.

Whichever it was, it doesn't matter. I succumbed to a weakness inside me and walked over to Sufi minding his own business with that luscious bone of his, grabbed it out of his mouth, and threw it over the wall and out into the street.

I don't remember if I went down to the road to retrieve the bone or if I left this disastrous situation hanging. I don't suppose that it matters. The damage was done. Maybe, Sufi didn't really know what happened. I am not an expert in the capacity of dogs to experience emotion. At the same time, I'm not so silly as to not recognize my own shameful behavior. Maybe, I thought that this bone-throwing would make me feel better.

In trying to turn this into a positive experience, perhaps the universe, in this situation, did align in order to show me something about myself that I could never have learned without Jeff's, Eric's, or Sufi's assistance. Whether I retrieved the bone or not doesn't change the reality of tearing it from Sufi's mouth and throwing it in the first place.

Some actions just can't be undone, however much we wish. I know it may sound sappy, but I certainly wish I could take this one back. Doing something ugly when we feel ugly inside never makes us feel better. This kind of act just makes us more aware of how hard we need to work on ourselves in order to prepare to be better partners for our future wife or husband and a better parent to our future sons and daughters. This is a story of which I'm truly ashamed, but one that needs to never be forgotten. Sufi was able to provide a foil for me to generate consciousness. This was his unconscious gift to me. In the same thinking, this is also Jeff's and Eric's gift to me, as well.

To place this all into context, this is the kind of lesson that speaks to an 11 year old. Most importantly, the dirt clods smashing into my pride, the sting of rejection by my peers, and my absolutely shameful behavior toward Sufi is a powerful lesson to shape a person's maturation that could never be conveyed in a classroom.

Speaking as an adult reflecting on something that happened 25 years ago, I hope that I don't throw metaphysical dirt clods at my wife and child, or any of my coworkers for that matter. And if I'm hit with one from time to time, I hope I've learned to not go ripping some loved object from another weaker person and destroying it in a fit of immature rage. This just doesn't feel like smart behavior that is conscious of the balance that creates healthy relationships.

I share this story because of how mundane it really is. I share this story in an effort to highlight how absolutely pervasive our learning is when couched in social interactions, or interpersonal intelligence. This intelligence, probably more than any other, is something that delivers some of our most immediate, as well as long-lasting, learning experiences. The absolutely scary thought, for an educator, is that these experiences exist at a more pervasive and fundamental level than anything we can hope to craft in a formalized social interaction in a scrubbed and manufactured environment such as a classroom.

On one hand, talking about this in a class, if it had never happened, would not have the same impact. Reflection is a powerful tool, but it only works if the individual, the student or teacher, has rich source material from which to craft an interesting discussion. Otherwise, the discussion methodology, as a valid learning experience, would be truly challenging. On the other hand, trying to craft experience into the classroom is problematic in that our actions and roles lose authenticity. The formal structure of the classroom scrubs much of the regular social intelligence from us. After all, classrooms and traditional education are based around an aesthetic that looks to logical and linguistic intelligence as the two most important qualities in humans that need to be continually shaped through a solidly designed and well-implemented curriculum.

Classrooms are problematic to the interpersonal experience. Teachers and students are constrained by the established roles that define behavior in a classroom. As an instructor and designer of educational experience, there really is no way that I would want to craft such a traumatic episode into one of my classes. That falls way outside my educational philosophy.

However, I want to express carefully that I look to my life to teach me and I want my students to be open to the same kind of education through experience of conscious social interaction. I feel personally called on to try to stimulate what my esteemed colleague, Dr. Daniel Janik, in his fascinating and accessible book "Unlock the Genius," calls the secondary learning pathway.

Just as Mr. Sun challenged me to move far afield of the English grammar book by engaging in intensely personal examination, I learned over time to bring this dynamic into my own classroom on a larger scale. I started in stages. I began by moving the desks around, away from the familiar straight rows, and working to create a personal space for the students. Once I arranged everything, the focus was not on me or on the front of the class. Instead, the students were focused on one another.

This made little sense to the other teachers who shared my classroom. After receiving a fair share of raised eyebrows, though, these teachers simply moved to another classroom and my little cave behind the elevator on the third floor became more and more

"Mr. O's classroom". Then, I started shifting my assignments to take advantage of the opportunities afforded by this new design.

While I was first hired to teach writing classes, I look back and shudder at my technique. I spent all week examining various essays and essay styles with the students, as a dutiful teacher would, before having each student create a five-paragraph essay during class each Friday. Over the years I recognized something: The more focused the reasoning and language, the greater the quality of the essays. I also noticed my great failure: The students had no confidence in their writing, even though their proficiency had sky-rocketed.

I was just mature enough as a professional, at the time, to recognize that this was a failure. There was no sense in sending out proficient writers into the world if the students had no belief in their skill. So, I began to play with the recipe. Instead of having every student write 10 complete essays during the quarter, I had the students participate cooperatively in the creation of 10 essays during the quarter. My hypothesis was that the students' confidence would rise as they interacted and witnessed the growth in one another.

To do this, I put the students in groups of three and four in which each student had a clearly defined role, such as leader, recorder, reporter, and timekeeper. The first cooperative assignment was usually designed to understand the purpose of prewriting. As a class, we would design the outline of an essay on a fun topic. Each group would be given a paragraph to write that fit the plan on the board. We called the plan a "map".

After fifteen minutes were used to write the paragraph, each of the reporters would come to the front of the room and arrange themselves in order, from thesis through body paragraphs to the conclusion paragraph. Beyond the laughs and camaraderie this kind of moment generated in the classroom, everyone walked away with a very real experience about why pre-writing is so important: Without it, we can easily forget what we want to say, meant to say, and get lost in a tangle of confusing sentences.

Equally important, each student saw in one another the frustration of becoming an effective writer. Through the cooperative learning exercise, each student realized that his or her teammates were also just beginning to engage forward momentum in life. After all, these students were not dumb. They knew that the ability to write had everything to do with career aspirations that were motivating their return to school. They were also aware that they would not become a success without engaging colleagues in a constructive and healthy manner.

I recognize that this is an education that is challenging to craft. I can challenge students to develop the consciousness of human dynamics through discussions of communication and analysis of successful interactions. However, there is more to a successful interpersonal intelligence than that which can be discovered in interaction. Silence plays an important part in our development of interpersonal sophistication. The interpersonal intelligence is best prepared by its sibling: the quality called intrapersonal intelligence.

"Intrapersonal intelligence involves the capacity to understand oneself, to have an effective working model of oneself- including one's own desires, fears, and capacities- and to use such information effectively in regulating one's own life"

~ Howard Gardner

Chapter 3

Intrapersonal Intelligence
Focusing Inwardly

Consider our own ways of expressing conflict. Each of us is different. Not only are we different from one another, but we are also different in our responses according to our own maturity, as well as because of our motivation and methods of interacting with the moment. Some of us want to talk out the issues as soon as conflict arises. We need the catharsis that comes with knowing that everything is going to be alright, even though disagreements occurred and feelings may have been hurt.

Others among us complain that the person they are in conflict with, or the conflict itself, just doesn't make any sense. We can't picture our behavior or the other person's behavior as problematic or downright insulting from another perspective beyond our own right away. Some of us might argue that the other's point just doesn't make logical sense. If we cannot track through another person's perspective in a clear and coherent way, then it is easy for us to dismiss this person's perspective as unworthy of reflection. These are all powerful biases which challenge us throughout our lives. I would contend that, to a large degree, our ability to move and grow from these experiences has everything to do with the success of our lives.

However, we respond to conflict in all of these ways at various times depending on our own state of mind. Furthermore, none of these responses are bad or wrong. In many ways, our dominant way of behaving in these intense situations of conflict is a tell-tale sign of our dominant intelligence at the moment of conflict. One of the most pervasive and common responses for many of us is to want to withdraw during a conflict so that we can reflect on the explosive moment before responding to the situation at hand. These responses can all be called expressions of our Intrapersonal Intelligence.

Rather than defining ourselves, as we often do, through our relations with others, this intelligence can only be understood through our cultivation of a rich internal world. This internal world is one which we begin crafting very early in life. We probably really began to notice it as we played with our toys as children and made fancy flights of imagination.

I certainly remember long hours spent in the sun as I built sand castles at the beach which were filled with knights, dragons, and secret chambers stuffed with esoteric knowledge. This same impulse grew into fanciful daydreams during elementary school. Any teacher or parent can describe the vacant look in a child who has floated into a place which is utterly pure and direct, but far from participatory. Far from being bad behavior or some kind of mental defect, this dreamy behavior is a fabulously important skill that assists us throughout our lives. In fact, entire traditions have made a point to craft this intrapersonal intelligence as an essential skill for consciousness. The Zen Buddhist tradition has a playful method which is passed from monk to monk harbored within strange riddles which have come to be known as koans. The first time I became aware of these koans was during my experience teaching in Korea.

One of the interesting contracts that I had the opportunity to work on was with the South Korean government. Somewhere along the way, the government decided that they wanted to introduce a highly structured curriculum using cooperative learning techniques for some of the high level government ministers. The concept was that each of the small learning groups made up of about 12 government ministers would move among teachers and activities throughout the course of the day. I jumped at the chance as this seemed to be an interesting opportunity for me to develop confidence as an instructor, as well as a real-world application of a formalized educational strategy.

Moreover, this was far away from the fascinating negotiations of culture and intellect I was enjoying every morning with Mr. Sun. Also, this environment was radically different than the freewheeling conversation classes stumbling along at the Police Academy and at the Tax Officer Training Institute which typically gained traction on conversations centered on weekend drinking binges and debates concerning whether Starcraft or World of Warcraft were better video games.

After winning participation in this lucrative contract, the few of us selected were required to attend some training during which our roles as instructors became defined. The entire curriculum was centralized around the cooperative learning model.

As it was described to us, cooperative learning is a strange but potentially effective learning model. Its strategies are excellent at developing small scale learning events in a highly controlled interaction. This model has grown quite prominent throughout the years, especially as the research into adult education has developed the realization that there needs to be a difference between pedagogy, a learning methodology for children, and andragogy, which is geared toward adults.

I remember the days moving one by one quite quickly during the 2 to 3 months I worked on this project. I had the distinct pleasure of driving in South Korea at this point in my adventure. Life was a blur. We would teach at the Police University or the Tax Officer Training Institute, pile into the car, race to the government center at Kwachon, and teach our cooperative groups. Then, we would pile back into the car and race to the next school, teaching sometimes as much as 9 hours a day.

The vignettes given to us by the curriculum developers at Kwachon, this government administrative area, included discussions that asked our learning groups to make triage decisions in emergency situations, to describe their emotional texture as described by mythical animals, and to make decisions as to the people that they believe might create a successful outpost on the moon. The most interesting one was based on a newspaper article that stated that the Korean bias towards male babies and the abortion of female babies had created an artificial imbalance in the population.

As it turned out, the newspaper article posited that the birthrate was so imbalanced that only 1 in every 5 babies was female. Furthermore, the article went on to discuss how this might affect a whole generation of Korean boys unable to find a wife. The discussion that day was thick with ideas about culture change.

I think the speed of this time was compounded by the mixed feelings I had for this educational experience. I think it was pretty clear to everyone that I didn't believe completely in what was happening there. As soon as the contract was finished, I was released and not asked to return for another term, despite solid reviews and good relationships with both the students and administrators. I don't regret it and am not embarrassed about it. The situation, however, offered me a radical juxtaposition of the fast and slow moments in my life.

We tend to think that speed goes slowly when we have conflicted feelings about our circumstances. I haven't felt this to be the case; the opposite seems to be true. Personally, time moves slowly when I dig in and concentrate on soaking through an experience.

Typically, these slow moments seem to be intellectually and sensually satisfying experiences. Sight, tastes, and smells can be conjured from moments which we choose to make matter. In the end, this fullness in experience is an essential part of fulfillment.

One day, just after a quick lunch in the cafeteria, I was enjoying a quick ray or two of sunshine before walking back into class. During the many lunches I enjoyed in Korean cafeterias, I noticed a very interesting cultural behavior. Everyone would eat all of their food first; then each person would walk outside where there was often a well with a pump. Each person would pump a single cup of water which was quickly gulped away and the cup replaced on a tray that would make its way back to the dish washer. Only rarely would a second glass be pumped.

While watching this very different dining style and musing on how something so simple has the ability to speak so loudly concerning the space that culture creates between human beings, I was called over to a group of men standing in the shade waiting for the afternoon session to begin.

Quickly, the appointed speaker for the group indicated that he wanted to ask me a question. He said, "Son Saeng Nim (teacher), may I ask you a question?"

Of course, I was happy to oblige, "Sure, what can I do for you?" I figured he was going to ask me some kind of obscure grammar question such as to why we have so many different predicate verb tenses that are poorly differentiated. This time, I received nothing of the sort.

"Do you know what a Zen koan is?" he asked.

"No."

"May I share one with you?"

I nodded my head and flashed him a smile to communicate my interest. He began to tell me the framework of the Zen koan. He explained it thus:

"Imagine that you are hanging from a branch of a tree by your mouth. You are hanging there with your hands and feet tied behind your back. The tree branch from which you hang is over a cliff. If you open your mouth, then you will fall to your death. Yet, someone is below the tree asking you a question to which you cannot help but respond. What will you do?"

I took a few seconds to absorb the picture, as I'd never heard of anything of the sort before. At the same time, something didn't strike me as quite right with the mental picture. I remember that time slowed down for a few breaths as I looked around. The shade sharpened.

"I would let go." After a pause, I then added, "I would let myself fall to my death." A quiet nod shifted their faces and our eyes connected.

One asked, "Why did you choose this outcome?"

"If the question is something that I cannot help but answer, then I can only identify one possible response: I must answer."

Another interrupted "But why would you not try to find some other solution?"

Shushing him, another spoke, "Why would you not then choose to simply hang forever?"

"In my mind, I cannot see that there is any way to answer the question, except with my words. If I don't answer the question, then I may hang for awhile. Eventually, though, I'll die. I am, just as we all are, human. Whether I answer the question or not, I die." I shrugged.

One of the men baited me, "So, what's the difference?"

I teased them, "I would prefer to live a fulfilled life, rather than one in which I simply hang around waiting to do something."

We laughed at that and returned quickly to our quiet enjoyment of the sun and cigarettes. Before long, we were called back to another class.

The memory evaporates after this, as I look back. I don't know if my response was appropriate to the koan. I don't know if this was a satisfactory response for these powerful men in charge of the day to day management of a country. I don't even know that it matters. I know very little about Zen. What I have been made to understand through my readings and discussions with practitioners of Zen seems to highlight the perspective that there is no definitive response to a koan. Zen, in general, seems to be a kind of system of ideas that is uninterested in assessment and evaluation and therefore uninterested in the framework of correctness or incorrectness, much to the chagrin of the Western thinkers so deeply invested in deductive processes and the measurement of quantifiable outcomes.

Instead, koans seem to be inductive learning experiences. Through this memory, this koan sneaks back into my consciousness often over the course of the last 10 years of my life, especially as I consider my professional development. As I move away from a core of teaching, I wonder if I am loosening my jaws' grip on the branch and am preparing to fall into a new beginning.

This feeling of excitement at the prospect of a new beginning steeping inside of me is certainly indicative of the Eastern influences permeating more and more through me, on a small scale, and through a much larger scale in the intellectual culture of the West.

I understood at that moment that the koan, as a puzzle in and of itself which was posed to me while I enjoyed that beautiful summer day with the South Korean government ministers over a decade ago, didn't matter. What I mean by saying that it didn't matter is not that it had no value; instead, I try to think of the koan as simply being an ingredient in a moment, just a part of a confluence of events that happened to bring a group of people together on a summer day representative of our peculiar combination of experience and biology. The koan was simply a little but profound truth-artifact to be shared among people respectful of each other sharing a peaceful moment.

At the same time, my response wasn't going to change their perspective of me as an individual, or of American culture. In this way, my response didn't matter. Even if these men remember our interaction as I do, they probably do not remember my name or my face.

The koan helped to craft a moment that was deeply honest, however. It challenged a group of individuals, who are representative of very different world views, to share a moment together filled with mystery, connection, and most importantly: learning.

Peering into the situated learning moment that arose due to the koan, I also realize that my response to the question posed in it is equally unimportant. What really matters in my unraveling of the koan is simply in the action of making a response to the question, to use its language, as I hang from my teeth over a precipice. I remember that the powerful message broadcast to me throughout my youth was that fulfillment came only through conscious and protracted struggle. Instead, my delightfully novice interpretation is that fulfillment is a gift that comes to us by merely showing up and being honest with ourselves, by allowing ourselves to fall with commitment into a moment.

Only through discipline applied throughout the minutes and hours of a life can we begin to show up and be honest. I'm sure that I'm not the only one who can look at myself in the mirror and acknowledge that there is always a more present and truthful version of me that needs to emerge. This is a challenge that I issue to myself every time I am lucky enough to engage another person, especially if the person looks to me for mentorship.

As a teacher, I have to dig deeply in order to not judge or define what success has to be. I realize this unwillingness to judge and define may fly in the face of how educators often see their role. For me, I try to think of my role in much the same manner as a researcher would. I try to identify where a person is in their development upon my first interaction. Then, I try to set up stages that allow for me to collect evidence concerning development. Finally, I work hard to give an honest appraisal of the evidence and come to some kind of idea of a grade. Often, I navigate another stage and seek to negotiate this assessment with the student by presenting my evidence and asking for further clarification.

On one hand, this process seems incredibly social. On the other hand, an intensely personal challenge is issued that must be answered only by turning inward and finding a quiet place to reflect upon the evidence collected throughout the trajectory of the class. These people have their futures riding on the grade which I will issue. It is only with great gravity that I issue my assessment. Thinking back to the koan, the students are hanging from the tree and I, as their teacher, am the one asking the question that they cannot help but answer. There is no other alternative but to recognize the deep spirituality of this role.

***

I made an odd decision at 12 years old. At the time, I was a quiet child with a spiritual bent. I liked to read and surf. Both can be quiet soulful journeys. I spent hours in my room pouring over stories and history and I always surfed all by myself. I liked paddling out into the ocean and sitting on my board quietly waiting and watching for the right wave to come my way. Instead of attending the local high school that was awash in sex, drugs, and all of those things that scare conscious children and parents, but dangers for which teenagers crave, I chose to leave my hometown with its beaches and sunburns and spend most of the next few years in a monastery out in the middle of nowhere.

I cannot defend this decision as being necessarily the greatest on my part. I certainly lost a few years in areas of my maturation in the process. While my parents did encourage the decision to attend the monastery school, they did not force me to pursue that path. I'm sure, however, that they were absolutely relieved that I had no interest at all in our local public high school. In fact, I can still hear their relief-filled exhale when I told them that I was okay with pursuing my education while living with the old monks on top of the hill.

If I had been aware enough, then I might even have called the thing going on inside of me a vocation. Whatever it was, I knew that it wasn't going to come to fruition so close to home. I was probably on the edge of being aware that I needed a bit of space from my parents and their powerfully intellectual world views in order for me to find my own way into this life. The dinner table in our house always mingled classical music, but never Beethoven—which gave Dad indigestion—and challenging examinations of daily life couched in the language of psychology and existential philosophy.

While I realize that making the decision to attend the monastery school in light of these comments about my family life may seem like heady thoughts for a 12 year old, I offer that all of this was not quite conscious at the time. Rather, it was as if I was improvising from a script that I only barely understood or even glimpsed, but that I knew was somehow essential for my independence.

This monastery school that I chose was not of any strange or esoteric cult. It was a training ground for the future priests of a very small and obscure Catholic order. While I was not Catholic, I was accepted into the community as long as I agreed to participate in all aspects of abbey life and to keep an open mind to a belief system that was different from my own. As I look back, I do not think that there was any way that I could exclude myself from any single part of the ritualized experience of that place without unraveling the entire experience.

Day in and day out, we followed a well-developed trajectory that challenged us both in a social manner, as well as in an internal and intrapersonal manner. At the time, this was lost on me, but I look back at the time spent there now with both awe of the powerful learning experience that transcended the lessons in the classroom and sadness that no child could ever understand the importance of these lessons until much later in life. The time I spent there on the mountaintop taught me that an education is never simply the stuff in the curriculum. I echo the sentiment of the great jazz musician, Miles Davis, who said that great music is always created in the space between the notes, in silence. In other words, beauty in action is crafted through conscious inaction.

Every morning, we would wake up in silence. We were not allowed to talk until after morning prayers. We would wake up, wash our faces, do chores, shower, get dressed, and then line up for the raising of our flags while remaining completely and utterly silent. Lined up in front of the flags, we were inspected to make sure that our belts were on, that we had matching socks, and that our ties were tied correctly and hung straight down with the ends as close to the belt as possible.

The first words out of our mouths every morning were the "Pledge of Allegiance." After this formal gathering and inspection, we walked to the church in silence and said morning prayers. These prayers were formalized and chanted. Each day, we opened our prayer books to the proper day and chanted a few lines.

After our chant, we sat in the darkened church for about 15 minutes before the simple closing ceremony. After exiting the church, we began our quiet rush along the walkway for the door of the dining room. In proper young-boy style, some jostling, elbowing, and stink-eye ensued, but no word was ever spoken. We knew that if any of the priests heard a peep from any one of us, then breakfast might never happen. Silence held serious importance for the ancient ones. It was not until the priests were seated with their food and had begun chewing that an audible sigh of relief would fill the dining room. It was only then that we were allowed to say our first independent words of the day.

At the end of the last class period, 9 p.m., we were allowed to socialize for a half hour. We often spent this time walking around the dormitory and enjoying a snack. On rainy nights, we probably found a quiet place in a classroom to hang out with our friends. After the bell rang, we all quietly lined up and walked into the church, carefully sitting down in rows according to class. After everyone was situated, we chanted our evening prayers with a repetitive cadence. We read off each line using a single note and ended the last syllable a fifth lower. Over and over, we read each line and dropped the last syllable a little lower until we finished the section.

Again, we were left to sit in quiet reflection. At night, this reflection period was much longer than the one which began the day. We would usually sit for anywhere between 35 minutes to a full hour. I was never sure if this was because the old priests would fall asleep or if this was on purpose. I remember squinting my eyes trying to figure out whether the ancients were still breathing. At the time, I'm sure that I didn't really understand the purpose of this exercise. These days, though, my mind has settled on the idea that this was a kind of meditation, a symbolic transition from our busy days into the quiet night.

Of course, as a teenager, I thought that all of this hocus pocus was a bunch of hooey. I used to tease the rituals as being all about the "bells and smells" because of the Catholic practice of ringing bells and burning incense as methods to heighten the drama of the ritual sacraments. Not only did I not really embrace this vow of silence every night, I probably spent a fair amount of the time trying to figure out how to talk with my friends after hours without getting in trouble. I certainly remember trying to sneak around and get away with turning the school into a slumber party.

At the same time, this silence was such an integral part of the culture of the monastery. I really couldn't avoid absorbing the significance of this quiet time just through my consciousness of it. It's not as if I could just give lip service and then act in whatever manner I wanted, as most of us do in the face of such rituals once we are out of earshot of the church.

After all, I never was out of the earshot of the church. So, this ritualized silence became something that, while I didn't understand or respect it, I certainly came to experience it as an essential part of my life and felt at home inside of the quietness it created throughout our community.

It hit me much later during my final semester at U.C. Berkeley, as I struggled to finish my Bachelor degree in the parentally-required 4 year time span. Due to my enjoyment of long summer vacations, my final semester required 20 units mixed with core classes and electives in order for degree completion. In an effort to try to lighten this load, I took electives like "B Movies of the '70s," a class on the philosopher-mystic Jiddu Krishnamurti, and, as a desperate measure to get myself up and at school every morning early: a class that was framed as a meditation hour.

I thought, until this time, that meditation was something exotic and mysterious that only old people from Asia practiced or old smelly hippies did while stoned or standing on their heads. This seemed, in my sort-of-conscious manner, as a great way to get going early every day; plus, there was a cute girl from my dorm taking it as well. Motivation is a strange thing. Thank God for that cute coed.

All joking aside, I recognize now what an essential part

meditation has had on my life, whether as a child on the beach ebbing and flowing with the waves, a budding musician spending hours bent over my instrument, or as an acolyte living in the quiet contemplative life of monastery ritual.

In hindsight, I would never have survived that final semester at Berkeley if I hadn't made the effort of sticking that class out and getting on campus bright and early every day. The class taught me that meditation is all about finding beginnings. Through mindfulness, I better recognized the origins of my breath, thought, and action.

***

Reflecting back to motivation, the psychology discussed by Viktor Frankl does much to color in the story of intrapersonal intelligence. By way of quick introduction, Frankl was a beautiful man and a very deep thinker who emerged after World War II. Much of his philosophy was developed as a direct result of the observations he made during his years as a prisoner in the infamous Holocaust death camps of Nazi Germany. In his work, he does a fine job of describing what kind of monstrous things that he witnessed, as well as discussing the essential freedom that exists within every human being.

During his time there, he noticed that in all of the people around him there was a light. This light is a metaphor that described each person's cause for living, a kind of internal nobility. This carefully nourished cause for living was the prisoners' freedom from that place, the prisoners' ability to see a life beyond the despicable things that were happening all around in these camps, a purpose that caused them to do what needed to be done to survive while enduring these brutal surroundings. As the years went on and he became more aware, Frankl noticed that every single one of his fellow prisoners were swallowed up by the death in these camps at the very moment that they lost their nobility, the ability to continue to dream, to find some freedom. He writes in a way that seemed to convey that it was almost uncanny how, when the prisoners lost their faith, the orders came for them to march into the gas chamber.

Through these observations, Frankl offered mankind one of the most beautiful realizations ever: that we, as conscious human beings, are not a simple stimulus-response system. We don't just have a single response to the things that happen to us. Our lives, in many ways, are crafted by our choice of responses to those events. While this stimulus-response system model may seem ridiculous to us now, immediately after World War II, this was a predominant perspective.

By focusing on this intensely personal space between what happens to us and our crafting of a response, we are free no matter the oppressive political system we live in or the squalor that threatens our very being each and every day. The freedom given to us by this gap between what happens to us and how we choose to respond is, as Frankl describes, a kind of power that cannot be denied to any human anywhere. He defines it as the center of our healthy thought.

Thinking about Frankl's perspective in terms of Gardner's theory, I would say that this description of our freedom is the root from which our intrapersonal intelligence grows. Furthermore, Frankl offers us a great understanding of the place in our minds where motivation lives. A clumsy metaphor for this is a garden. The gap that Frankl describes is the place divided for each bulb, or seed, and put aside as a place for allowing something to grow. Motivation is the soil. It has to be rich and nourishing. And, as when the garden's space and the soil mix successfully, intrapersonal intelligence is the life which grows out of the ground and reveals its fecundity in our lives by offering us rich interpretations of our behavior, its sources, and its effects on others around us.

Of course, just as a plant cannot grow larger than the pot in which it has been planted, so can our intrapersonal intelligence's growth also be stymied. The challenge is for us to find ways to expand the space between absorbing the world and formulating a reaction. If Frankl speaks of a freedom that occurs in the space between that which happens to us and our response to the world, then the challenge for those of us seeking to live more conscious lives is to always work on pushing back the response time to allow for the emergence of a richer interior monologue. Meditation, in all of its guises, is about the development of intrapersonal intelligence and the growth of this freedom that Frankl described.

Looking back to my experiences in the monastery, the meditation class, and later as I explored Korea, I realize that a cultivation of conscious space was the purpose of those quiet moments which we crave during the busy times in our lives. An opportunity for reflection allows us to find out why we are doing what we are doing, whether our behavior is getting us what we want, and if a subtle shift in our actions might better align our external world with what's going on inside each of us every minute of every day.

In the monastery, we sat in the church every night soaking in an opportunity to take a second and slow down the speed of our life. The priests obviously were well aware of this even though we knew nothing of their long-range goals for us. The silence was designed for us to cultivate some kind of internal monologue that would serve us later in life as our careers started picking up speed and as we began to raise our own children.

As an instructor and university administrator, I've dabbled in bringing this into the classroom, especially into the classes filled with students pursuing high-stress work, like business students and students working in high technology. I can see that they must think that the whole experience of meditating is bizarre and weird at first. The look on each face is the same one that was on my face while sitting in a cold dark church looking to see if the old priest was still alive. It is my wish that these students, whom I am now responsible to assist along the trajectories of their unique lives, have a moment for the cultivation of their own personalities, not just their technical skills. We cannot just attend school for the shallow and pragmatic efforts afforded us by content expertise.

Zachary M. Oliver

"Musical intelligence entails skill in performance, composition, and appreciation of musical patterns"

~ Howard Gardner

Chapter 4

Musical Intelligence
Melody, Harmony, and Rhythm

Dreaming of those early days in the kindergarten classroom sitting in those nice rows of desks neatly facing the front of the room, I remember happy teachers who encouraged us to explore our environment. While the sun streamed in from big glass windows looking out onto a giant lawn and our favorite jungle gym, our days were full of play as we reached out to begin our first real forays into socialization and formal learning.

We were allowed to run around and behave as children. At the same time, we were presented with an environment that challenged us to engage other children in some very significant ways. In order to prepare us for these encounters in a social world, the teachers had some strategies that they knew would stick in our excited little minds. One of the most pervasive, taking some of our time each day, was the memorization and singing of songs.

One of the most anticipated parts of the day, for me, was circle time. During circle time, we always sat on the floor cross-legged and practiced our songs. We sang with our little hearts full of life. In return, the songs filled our minds with precious meaning, the acceptable and culturally-digested information that would be used to jump-start some of our more complex cognitive processes.

This was the beginning of a framework on which our entire intellectual future would be built.

An obvious example is our alphabet song. I'm sure that I'm not alone in remembering my ABC's through the melody of a happy song that still haunts me every time I have to alphabetize anything. To this day, I have to sing the song to navigate my way through the alphabet. I'm sure that my preschool teacher never would've dreamed that I'd ever write a book.

The songs didn't stop with the alphabet. We also made songs that taught us about knotting our shoe laces. I was never very good at that song, but my daughter mastered her knots while chanting the lyrics to a strange tale of a bunny circling around a hole over and over.

Using the vivid pictures of imaginary animals and situations, sometimes just a catchy melody, these songs taught us the rudiments of many things that we'd need to know later in life. Songs were very successful at teaching us vocabulary about this world which we were just beginning to experience. A whole generation knows all about this from a song about the wheels of a bus, which hypnotically go round and round.

In much the same way, we learned, during these early times, short little sing-song poems called nursery rhymes. From them, we learned about how to make and treat friends, how to share, why parents should be respected, and much of the acculturation on which much of our adult world is built. We learned about Humpty Dumpty, Old MacDonald and his dog, Bingo, and even about the existence of black sheep. Each of these characters taught us something: The black sheep taught us about the sounds that animals make and that, as we become more complex in our thinking, it is important to share what we have with those who have less. The black sheep has a bag for the master, the dame, and for the little boy down the lane.

As we became more advanced, Humpty Dumpty taught us that our acts have finality. What we do in this life affects us. We need to think things out. Furthermore, if we don't, then the results are often negative. After all, "all the king's horses and all the king's men couldn't put Humpty together again."

Once the alphabet was old news, Old MacDonald and his dog, Bingo, helped us improve our spelling. Sometimes, especially in those last minutes before recess, it was really hard to remember which letter we were on as we chanted through the verses, each one asking us to drop another letter from Bingo's name. If we made a mistake, then we would have to sit out the rest of the song. And this was not a fun way to end the song.

These songs and nursery rhymes trigger a very basic and profound intelligence: our musical intelligence. There is something magical about music for so many of us. A great melody has the power to uplift us regardless of our mood. The right rhythm at the right moment can make even the coldest heart start beating with passion until a foot taps, a head nods, and a butt wiggles. Music connects our mind with our body in a very visceral way. Music is real and direct in a way that not much else is.

Any musician who has spent real time with his or her instrument knows of the focus that emerges. We work our fingers up and down trying to find a new pattern that speaks to us in a new language. After fussing over our technique for hours on end, we can stand up refreshed and excited, almost ebullient, over a breakthrough. Sometimes, we can spend month after month preoccupied with a section of a song which refuses to leave our conscious but for when we sleep. Yet, we never tire of these long sessions which afford us hours of relentless attention on the tiniest quivers of a practiced vibrato which brings the end of a phrase of the catchy melody into focus. When everything comes together, we can feel that vibrato extend outwards to the corners of the room and reflect back to us at just the right speed.

A great way to think about this mind-body connection is in the reflection, as discussed in other parts of this story, of our own behavior while facing boredom. Boredom is no stranger for most of us facing another long afternoon in school. Instead of focusing on the travesty that is an education system that causes students to face boredom on a regular basis, the classroom full of these bored students offers an interesting laboratory in which human behavior might be studied.

The collection of behaviors in such a classroom runs the gamut of each of the intelligences and often two, three, or more at once. Music is often the externalized expression of our intelligence which helps to connect us back into a situation which triggers boredom, whether because of a lack of meaningful input or because of our lack of capacity to deal with the overwhelming amount of input. Music offers us respite, a safe place to escape to until we can get a grip, click back into reality, and get traction in a big and complex world.

The musical intelligence can be witnessed in the girl with the pony tails absent-mindedly humming the lyrics to the newest hit song during math class or in the boy tapping his foot rhythmically and accompanied by a pencil in his hands used to carefully punctuate a syncopated multi-rhythm with an eraser bumping against a closed schoolbook.

The multitude of teenagers learning rock and roll songs on beat-up guitars is representative of the joy of music and its connection with our wish to distance ourselves from overwhelming emotional and intellectual stimulus. Judging by the onslaught of MP3 players and iPods which each hold thousands of songs spanning the centuries from Bach to Chopin and from Muddy Waters to Metallica, working adults on their way to and from work are not immune to the coping mechanism of putting on a set of headphones and tuning out the turmoil of the world for a few minutes.

Gardner talks about musical intelligence in his Theory of Multiple Intelligences as being separate from linguistic intelligence. He cites examples of people who have suffered brain injuries who have lost the ability to speak, but have retained the great joy of music. For Gardner, this was proof enough that these two skills, while seemingly related and intertwined, come from very different places, both figuratively and literally.

The research being presented in the biological sciences interested in human development and in cognition have some very interesting ideas to share.

It's well-known that the fetus lives in a richly sonic world. The fetus listens to and is comforted by the heartbeat of the mother. Research tells us stories of fetuses that respond to the mother's voice. Furthermore, we have all heard of the music that is marketed to eager parents that is said to engage the prenatal brain and encourage its development. Putting all these claims aside for a moment, it would seem safe to say that, if nothing else, sound is one of the first senses that the human fetus experiences. Furthermore, the sound of the mother's rhythmic heartbeat creates a sense of well-being and safety for the baby as it comes to term inside the mother's womb.

Some psychologists have also talked about how music

recreates the sensation of motion for us. This concept seems pretty straightforward when considering the dual roles our ears play in our successful navigation of our world. Biology, specifically the anatomical structure of the ear, backs up this assertion. Because our inner ears are used both for processing sound into the brain as well as maintaining balance, there is some physiological evidence that music tricks our brain into experiencing movement.

Ears are obviously our tool for listening to the world. It also happens that our ears are used to gauge our equilibrium. This is why, when we have ear infections or sinus colds, we feel off balance and woozy. Balance is essential for our ability to walk, to travel. The interesting thing about this, from an educator's standpoint, is that a body in movement is usually accompanied by an alert mind.

Observe a squirrel, mongoose, or even a bird. These creatures stop quickly to grab food or perhaps something useful for building shelter, twitch their heads to listen to the environment, and then look to see if there are threats close by. Then, each runs off or jumps into flight just as quickly as possible. For each, movement equals safety.

Deep inside our minds, we are not so different. Consider a distant past without our creature comforts, our central heating, refrigeration, and plumbing systems which are just a few of the technological achievements featured in our towns and cities which are often critiqued as monuments to our pursuit of control. Consider a world where we were once also prey, conscious of every movement in our vicinity and aware that our own ability to move gave us safety and some control over a dangerous world. From a practical perspective, a dangerous world is one full of things that are not understood.

While the world of a student is not necessarily physically dangerous, the effect of the available information certainly can shake preconceptions, the ground on which lives are built. Investigations into literature filled with rebellious philosophies and challenging theories are disquieting, to say the least. Anything we can do to ease the sense of danger that boils in us when our preconceptions are being challenged is truly welcomed. Music is one of the most direct tools that bring us back into focus and filled with a sense of safety. While it can be described in an intellectual manner, music is primarily a visceral experience experienced as a kind of wave which we allow to wash over us and to which we respond in an emotional manner.

This idea of immersing a student into a musical world without the traditionally intellectual vocabulary to describe the music is not new. An entire school of music instruction is based on the principle of listening. The Suzuki Method, based on the philosophy of Shin'ichi Suzuki, was designed to allow students to immerse their ears in the music, without becoming preoccupied with the more technical concerns of the instrument. By not clearly defining a technical curriculum, it seems that Suzuki knew that if a student is placed in a rich environment full of sound, then that student will work tirelessly in an attempt to organize that environment, to make a map of the unknown. While certainly not without its fair share of criticism, there are some exciting parallels that can be made between Suzuki's method and Gardner's concept of musical intelligence.

As an immature 6 year old, I began playing music through the Suzuki method. I learned to play the piano quite quickly through this school of ear-training. While quite young, I remember becoming quickly fascinated with Bach's Minuets, which are quite complex short compositions, and began playing them over and over in an attempt to make sense of the wonderful sound of each. I would sit behind my great-grandmother's lovely Wurlitzer and focus my entire attention throughout in an effort to make my fingers speak the music that I would listen to on the various tapes and records in my parent's music collection.

The ear-training became really useful to me throughout my teenage and young adult years as I struggled to teach myself how to play the guitar, which was far cooler than the piano at the time. Being able to immerse myself in the sound of the music because of my Suzuki training, I was able to pick up the instrument and sit down next to a radio and play songs after just a single time listening through it. Luckily, pop songs are typically pretty simple. Coming full circle, though, the really interesting thing about this learning style is that, twenty years after discontinuing my piano lessons, I have been known to sit down at a piano and be able to work my way through a Bach Minuet completely by memory. The astounding thing about this ability is the effectiveness of the learning, not my memory.

During my time as an instructor at a small private college in Honolulu, I taught many classes that would be called "developmental." This means that these classes were designed to address shortfalls between what students should know upon entering college and their actual skill, as tested by fancy standardized tests given just before the students begin school. The fancy term is "matriculate."

Primarily, I taught grammar, sentence structure, and paragraph development. My class was not the most interesting from the perspective of a student really more interested in learning computer networking or medical assisting, especially not at eight in the morning or eight at night.

Quarter after quarter, I watched students walk in and out of my classroom with headphones on, humming along to some pop song, and tapping beats with anything that could be turned into drum sticks. During my first few classes, I spent considerable energy asking students to put away headphones, stop tapping, and to be quiet out of consideration for their fellow colleagues. I thought these were the expectations for a functional classroom. Unfortunately, these simple requests were always received negatively, generated an antagonistic interaction that I then felt responsible to repair, and destroyed any momentum for the learning taking root among the students.

It hit me: One day, I walked into class with a big CD player. Everyone's eyes bugged and there was a strange murmur through the students. They asked, "So what, Mistah, you gonna make us listen to some whack classical music or what?"

"No, I was thinking that maybe I would play some Bob Marley. You guys like Mistah Marley better than Mistah Oliver anyways..."

While everyone laughed at my self-deprecation, they all understood a shift was taking place in our relationship. I was no longer the stuck-up haole teacher talking down to them while teaching them some concepts that were hard, boring, and slippery. Once the first couple of chords rang out and the students heard Bob Marley tell everyone that everything is going to be alright, the extra headphones got put away, they all started humming the same song, instead of three or four different songs, and all the tough boys were tapping beats that fit together instead of listening only to a beat inside of their own head.

All of a sudden, we were together, focused, and alert. For the first time, I really felt like a successful teacher. Everyone walked out of class that day with a shifted perspective about what a class could feel like and how learning might occur. The school buzzed with the news of the music and of the discussion that had surfaced that day.

Needless to say, the academic affairs department didn't really understand at first. They were worried. I noticed that deans started walking by my classroom daily peeking in to find out if this was really a class or if everyone was just playing around. A few complaints about noise were made, but no accuser actually stepped forward to address these issues with me personally.

So, I kept it going. Music was soon established as a featured element of the Mr. Oliver classroom experience. I started showing fantastic results on the tests assessing the students' grammar skills. The class was working through the concepts with greater speed, higher focus, and more enjoyment than ever before. The typical grind of teaching, the push/pull cycle of burnout and revival, quickly disappeared as I realized that I was enjoying myself as well.

My colleagues, those teaching the other sections of the same class, would complain that there weren't enough weeks in the quarter to teach the mechanics of the language. This was not my experience at all. These students, who had been labeled as developmentally deficient, were finished with the parts of speech within a week, independent and dependent clauses took another week, more complex punctuation and sentence construction followed up as we began to construct paragraphs. Because the students were learning the concepts more effectively and more quickly, we were all able to pace new learning more successfully and spend a lot of time circling back to reinforce previous knowledge.

The whole process began to feel like a game. We would roast each other playfully for getting our dependent clauses wrong. We would write sentences that were inane and often slightly disgusting. There were a lot of laughs. Retention started to go up. Pretty soon, the deans were making class visits twice and three times a quarter trying to figure out what was happening. These changes didn't happen all at once. But, once the boom box appeared, a lot of the shifts began to occur in our classroom.

Often, the deans would walk in the door and stand there, at the entrance, confused for a moment. Maybe, they were trying to figure out what to complain about first. Maybe, they were just trying to comprehend a very different kind of learning environment.

First, there was music playing. Typically, it was music that had a beat that could be used for dancing. Often, it was pretty clear that the students didn't care who was walking in or out of the class. They were absorbed in their activities. This must have been odd treatment for these deans. They were probably used to classes coming to a full stop upon their entrance. Typically, as they told me later, they would walk into a class conscious that the teacher was performing just for them and everything in the class, both the room and the students, were just "so."

This was not the case in my classroom. The classroom always looked to be in disarray. Newspaper articles, photos, and quotes were stuck to the walls by students wishing to share some piece of discovered wisdom with anyone wanting to investigate. Students were often walking around, desks were pushed together in odd ways, and the board was always in the process of being filled with strange codes that could be turned into sentences by those initiated into Mr. Oliver's grammar method. In the midst of all of this, I would prowl around the class calling for examples by name.

All of this energy, this magic, started by watching the students and recognizing that they, just like me, love music and want it to be part of their environment, feel more active and alert while enjoying a good song and, strangely, more relaxed while enjoying a solid beat and catchy melody. I had the best results, oddly, with reggae and smooth jazz, as long as the beat wasn't too slow. The students liked music with a little dance to it while studying. Instrumental music or music with really familiar lyrics, such as Bob Marley's songs, or lyrics that weren't really obtrusive, worked well.

Somewhere along the way, I decided that this was worth some research. So, I invited my colleague, who was working on a master's thesis, into the class to do some research on what the students thought about music in the classroom. She also tracked down former students who had experienced my noisy classroom and who had some time to let their ideas gel about it.

Avoiding all of the problems with methodology and sampling and all of the research complexity, it was interesting to find out that the students reported that they felt that music enhanced their experience, increased their attention, and helped them to retain the subject matter better and for longer. As more and more surveys came back detailing the students' perspectives concerning the inclusion of music in the classroom environment, I became more and more aware that this musical environment was a fundamental part of what was happening inside of them that allowed for them to feel more connected to a set of concepts which had always frustrated them. This relaxed and comfortable state assisted them in successfully incorporating correct grammar and usage into their writing.

It was sometime during this evolution of our classroom that I became aware of Gardner's Theory of Multiple Intelligence. Upon becoming familiar with it, and being impressed with its academic rigor and credentials, I felt relieved. This was not some crazy idea upon which I'd stumbled. This was an acceptable method to engage learners supported by an eminent researcher from Harvard University.

I cannot begin to relate how relieved I was that I wouldn't have to come up with an argument all by myself to express how important I thought this development was for my classroom. Furthermore, I was even more excited to see that Gardner expressed eight whole distinct intelligences that we all share which could be tapped into in much the way I had already begun. During the next few months, I realized that I was actually intuitively doing much to engage our learners through the use of strategies that worked with each of the other multiple intelligences in addition to the musical one.

Although I have left that position and have moved on to involve my professional energies on the development of faculty and program culture, I do hope that these students all learned a valuable lesson, as I have. Music glued us together. We listened, worked, and teased one another as we became an effective community. Learning became something that naturally developed out of our interactions once we, as students and teachers, stopped looking at each other antagonistically. Music helped us to ease our minds and recognize that successful learning environments are full of stimulus, not just four walls filled with silence.

"The naturalist is comfortable in the world...and may well possess the talent of caring for, taming, or interacting subtly with various living creatures"

~ Howard Gardner

Chapter 5

Naturalist Intelligence
Interaction with the Natural World

While I recognize and appreciate that people connect with the natural world in very different ways and with very different environments, such as by appreciating verdant valleys, craggy mountains, and crisp deserts, the sandy beaches, and especially the ocean with its boiling currents really communicate the beauty of the natural world for me.

To this day, I can sit on the beach and stare out at the ocean for hours as it moves and flows, glitters and glows. In those moments, I feel as if I am part of something much larger than myself. I feel engaged. My brain feels energized. I think better, clearer, and with more focus. This sharpness comes from a connection my brain feels with the natural world in all of its interwoven relationships. In these moments, it's hard not to perceive the world as a living creature, Gaia, the Earth embodied as a single organism which supports all life fostered in its ecosystems.

As a young boy, I grew up around the ocean, first in California and then in Hawaii. I've spent many days enjoying the beaches that are so much a part of the identity of both of these beautiful places. One of the things I love is to stand on a pier, some big rocks, or on top of a cliff and stare out at the surfers as they ride the powerful waves. Even now, as a busy professional, I still need moments during which nothing is planned and I can enjoy the sun on my skin, the wind through my shirt, and the sound of the waves roaring across a reef. This ritual of mine refreshes me.

The crashing waves have called out to me ever since I can remember. The art of riding waves has been so much a part of my life that some of my earliest memories are of running up and down in the tidal surge alternately splashing and screaming.

In fact, my earliest memory is sitting in a stroller taking a walk out on the pier with my grandmother. I was carrying a little silver Tonka truck, a Jeep, on a wonderful sunny winter day. I remember looking down into the green ocean, mesmerized by the vibrations of the waves moving through the pier's pilings. My little hand reached out through the railings holding the silver jeep for a moment before I let go and watched it drop down the fifteen feet to the water's surface. I didn't cry or get upset; I remember watching it sink quickly out of sight. Perhaps it was an offering to a world that would play a big part in my development as a person.

This love of the beach grew as I moved through my childhood and into adolescence. Surfing was a major part of my early life. As long as I could be out there amongst the breaking waves I never cared what kind of board I was riding, whether a body board, performance surfboard, or longboard. If I didn't have a board, then my belly was just fine too. What really caught me about surfing was the powerful intellectual connection with the environment that it inspired. Really, this connection can be more correctly described as a spiritual calling.

All of us who understood the calling would meet up in the dark, before the sunrise, and excitedly converse about the tide, the swells, and what kind of prevailing wind might grace us upon daybreak.

I had to adapt and learn about the confluence of tides, winds, and swells. These were strange equations that I had to decipher in order to be able to stand proudly as a true soul surfer. I developed a really strange but powerfully applicable perspective about the environments which I inhabited. I ran the algorithms in my mind over and over, trying to fathom why some beaches would break perfect waves one day and be flat the next. While I may not have been the most successful student in science class, I certainly learned a few things while floating among the crashing waves. My brain was far more active and entranced in this real and dynamic ocean world than it was in any of the classrooms where I eventually had to dry off in order to enter.

In fact, as I look back, I feel as if I lived a whole day before morning college classes ever started.

One of the major fascinations a surfer develops is with tides. Tides deeply affect the surfer's experience in a most direct manner. One can show up to a beach and watch, over the course of an hour, a profound change in the speed and strength of the waves. Beaches shift and change minute by minute. At any spot on any given day, the old surfers all wax philosophical about the mysterious communion between time and tides.

It was only later that I was exposed to the fact that the Moon is what urges the water towards shore at high tide and draws it away at low tide as it orbits around the Earth. I only learned later that tides grow and wane according to the lunar cycles, especially at the equinoxes and solstices. The knowledge was already visceral for me by the time I learned the theoretical framework in the classroom.

If I didn't already have a connection with the ocean through my love of surfing, then I would've never come to understand the complex interactions that connect the ocean with the heavens. Surfers know that there is no constant in the moving equation of tides, winds, and swells when in pursuit of the perfect wave. The surfer's mind must stay active computing the influence of each variable on his or her experience.

I remember waking up really early in the morning to catch the offshore wind which rushes off the land and onto the ocean. It holds up the waves and makes them stand up longer before breaking. On one hand, this is great if there is a strong surge from the ocean. On the other hand, this is horrible, as I found out by a few wasted early mornings, if there is no swell or an unhelpful tide.

In the later morning and into the afternoon, the common breeze turns around and rushes off the ocean onto the coast. This is called onshore wind. From a surfer's perspective, this can be damaging. The onshore wind pushes the waves over and creates choppy conditions. But if there are no waves, then the onshores, if combined with the right tide and coastal features, might actually stir up some solid, albeit choppy, waves.

Again, I eventually learned in class about the pattern of weather called convection. I remember laughing about it when the teacher brought it up. I thought she was talking about the oven in the kitchen called a convection oven. Despite the unfortunate trouble I probably got into for my lack of restraint, I did enjoy learning that there was a technical discussion about what I had worked for so long to implicitly understand.

I learned that the offshore breeze is caused because the ocean heats up faster than the land. Air rises off the ocean more quickly than off the land in the early morning. The land continues to get hotter than the ocean while the sun is shining. The land cools more quickly than the ocean during the night and takes longer to heat in the morning, but it catches up with the temperature of the ocean quickly. As the air rising off the land leaves an empty void below, the cooler and denser ocean rushes in to take its place.

I learned that we know this rising air phenomenon as part of the ability for big birds to float forever without flapping their wings and as the force that allows hang gliders to float endlessly, always circling higher and higher. I would have never learned any of this if I hadn't first found a basis in my direct experience of surfing and observing the beautiful environment where the ocean meets the land.

***

The story of the ancient Hawaiians really sets the tone for a discussion on the Naturalist Intelligence. The Hawaiians, after all, have an astonishing legacy. Before the time of GPS, Fed Ex, and motor boats, this group of people had the temerity to climb into an open air canoe and set off to find a new world. The construction of these canoes was genius. Each was completely made, assembled, and given propulsion with natural materials. Every detail was fussed over and thought through so that the individuals on this canoe would be provided the greatest opportunity for a successful and long life as the group struggled to find a new island on which to build a new culture. Wood, leaves, and vines were all twisted, bent, and formed to give opportunity for a group of individuals to pursue a dream written in the stars.

On each of these handmade canoes were stored between 20 and 30 plants that could be used to seed a whole new culture.

These people understood the bare minimum necessary that they needed in order to carry on the essential practices of their culture and the sustaining of human life. There was, after all, no FedEx that these people could use to send boxes of stuff that would wait for them patiently on a doorstep. They couldn't jump on the Internet, order curry powder from India or organically grown Basil from a certified grower in Argentina, and sit back in their Lazy Boy chair and watch a couple of movies while waiting for their ingredients to arrive.

The immensity of this reality cannot be understated. I can't imagine going out to a garden and picking out 25 plants that can be used to generate all of the food, medicine, and raw materials needed for a new culture to start. In fact, I don't even possess the skills necessary to successfully grow 25 plants in a garden. My skills end at the supermarket checkout line when I whip out my credit card.

Consider the reality of the Hawaiian ecosystem before human beings arrived. From what we know, there were no palm trees. These were brought in the first canoe. Not only were there no coconut trees in Hawaii before humans, but the islands were covered with nothing more than knee-high shrubs. This is a far cry from the rain forests that cover them now.

The natural environment of Hawaii in our time is actually not natural. It is man-made. We crafted it by introducing plant after plant, tree after tree. Hawaii is so remote that only a single species of plant and animal arrived here every 20,000 years. These plants and animals enjoyed fertile soil and little competition; so each would differentiate and evolve separately depending, for example, on whether the ancestor settled close to the water or further up the mountain. The wildlife that has been introduced to Hawaii has choked out many of the original inhabitants of the islands because the foreign species were much more accustomed to competition. The new plants and animals eat more and reproduce more often. In Hawaii, fertility is everywhere.

Beyond the plants and animals introduced by these first visitors to the islands, the Hawaiians used a fascinating navigation method as they sailed across the ocean looking for a new homeland. They read the stars. The Hawaiians knew how to use the stars as an old-school GPS system to watch the direction and speed of the canoe so that they could have a basic idea of where they were in the vast expanse of the ocean. They located the unmoving reference point called Hokulea, the star known to the western world as Polaris.

When I look up into the night sky, I see a lot of stars. Some are bright; some are dim. I recognize a few constellations, but only incidentally. I never stare long enough to find the pivot point around which all of these constellations seem to move.

Thanks to Hokulea, these ancient Hawaiians knew exactly where to look for each of their constellations and used the information available to them from the heavens to understand time of year and deduce regular storm and wind patterns. The attention to detail necessary to identify and code which constellations are rising and setting is, to put it quite succinctly, astounding.

As these seafaring people arrived on these profoundly beautiful islands, they must have marveled at the sensitivity and focus of their navigator and leader. I can imagine the feeling of being on a boat for weeks wondering if land would ever come into sight. I can imagine the feeling of smelling land over the horizon. Sometimes in the local bars, I hear stories of sailors describing the smell of land as intoxicating. I can imagine the green mountains slowly rising out of the sea as the canoe drew nearer to the island. Once on land, these ancient Hawaiians quickly transformed the ecosystem of the entire island with the plants and animals that were transported on the canoe for the express purpose of seeding this new burgeoning human society.

The amazing thing for me is that these people introduced each plant to the island in such a manner that human society could be fostered. These are all actions possessed by a clear thinking and highly intelligent group of people.

These stories aren't all that far from our experience even if we have no connection with surfing or with Hawaiian culture. Many of us can remember the long boring days stuck in a classroom while a sunny day was happening right outside. It took all of our spirit to stay in our seat. Despite knowing that punishment would be forthcoming, our eyes have this automatic impulse to move away from the green chalkboard or whiteboard and fixate on the tree just on the other side of the big window in the classroom. We try to see the leaves moving in the light breeze. Perhaps a little squirrel or bird might stop and look into our eyes. In a fit of anthropomorphy, we might imagine that it is wondering why anyone would be so silly as to sit inside on such a beautiful day.

Regardless of how good a teacher might lecture or how important a lesson is for our future, we need new stimulus, something more varied to look at, than a simple green chalkboard. The outside world offers us a complex and beautiful texture full of movement and stimulus. It has the ability to refresh a tired mind. Some researchers say that this is linked with our long history in nature. We are built with the need for this kind of stimulation. After all, our preoccupation with concrete and steel isn't more than a couple of hundred years old.

We have a long history in which we spent our human existence close to nature. Even a hundred years ago, most Americans lived on farms. Our economy was agrarian. While Americans have, to a large degree, moved away from the rural past, many other areas of the world are still full of people that feel the tug towards a life closely tied to nature. My wife's father, for example, made a hard decision. He is an old Korean man who has seen much in life. As a young man he survived the Korean Conflict. Afterwards he was offered, due to his fine academic achievements, a scholarship to study to become a doctor in the big city. Being a doctor did interest him deeply, but there was a deeper tug working inside him challenging him to take a different path.

Instead of moving to the city to study for a degree in medicine, he settled into life as a farmer. He says that he loved the smell of dirt. He talks about his plants as if they were his children. This man is clearly intelligent. He chose to walk away from a career which, in our society, seems to be a benchmark for intelligent individuals in order to feel fulfilled by a life that we, using the same benchmarks, would typically consider anachronistic and unsuccessful, yet close to nature.

Reflecting back to my memories of growing up on the beaches of Hawaii and California, I can appreciate the connection that this man feels with nature. I can understand that his intelligence is deeply involved in a very immediate way with his success. After all, his mind must be filled with equations much like mine, except that his are less interested in tides and swells. His are focused on the smell of a rain storm rising in the distance. His equations include pieces of information about how much water will be flowing from the reservoir and how dry the coming months might be.

In his mind, he must be constantly calculating the dynamic between the quality of the soil, the presence of insects and critters, and a whole set of additional variables. Any failure to take all of these bits of information into account for him is much more profound than a wasted trip to the beach. For him, any mistake in factoring out these equations means that his family wouldn't eat.

Zachary M. Oliver

"Spatial intelligence features the potential to recognize and manipulate the patterns of wide space (those used, for instance, by navigators and pilots) as well as patterns of more confined areas (such as those of importance to sculptors, surgeons, chess players, graphic artists, or architects)"

~ Howard Gardner

Chapter 6

Visual-Spatial Intelligence
Visual Representation

  Thinking back to my time in Korea, I realize how visually stimulating the whole experience was. I remember wandering around the commercial districts of the big cities surrounded by neon signs blinking with bright colors advertising what was happening inside. An ultra-modern world, it induced an almost trance-like state. I don't know if it was the electricity sizzling in the air or the hundreds of colors flying into my eyes second by second. On every floor of the buildings I saw bars stacked on top of restaurants stacked on top of cram schools stacked on top of custom suit tailors stacked on top of flower shops, creating a barrage of light as each of these signs would fight for its moment in the consciousness of the passerby.

  Along with the light is the mind-numbing beat of a thousand different techno textures blasting from every radio inside of each of these vertically stacked businesses. Ambient and mechanical, this music set the tone for an assault on the senses. While it may be overwhelming to those coming from a different world, such as myself, the people that live there surprisingly treat this as absolutely normal and think nothing of it.

  Thanks to the discos that play the same beats everywhere in

the world, I was prepared for the music. However, I certainly wasn't prepared for the powerful assault of this visual stimulation on my eyes. For the most part, my world is blue and flat. Hawaii's horizons are smooth; the cities are small and fairly low key. We've got green mountains that reach up, but not too high. By quickly scrambling to the top of the right one, we enjoy views of the ocean on three sides.

There are jungles that are graced by overgrown plants with leaves as big as a person and flowers that could be only described as obscene in their overt sensuality. There are little bubbling brooks fed by rain in the mountains graced with moss-covered rocks. There are deep black lava rocks that cut the tender feet of tourists, which we local people quickly dance across unscathed. I come from a quiet world filled with acoustic guitars, ukuleles, and soft harmonies.

Beyond the many hours spent at the beach staring out at the softly glittering and undulating ocean, I was lucky enough to spend my youth traveling. This offered me the opportunity to open my perspective to more than just the idyllic worlds which I was lucky enough to experience day to day.

Traveling does wonders for self awareness. It made me aware of a deeply ingrained friction within me. In a way, I'm a half-breed. I have a foot deeply planted in the American experience. My father comes from a family that defined the agrarian roots of America; he was raised on a dairy farm. His childhood memories include stories of drinking milk straight from the cow and learning how to churn butter. From my mother, my other foot stretches across the Atlantic Ocean to Europe, an older world which seems to continually and consciously celebrate the richly aesthetic experience of human life, especially the visual experience.

My parents met in post-war Europe. It's a classic story; their eyes met in a streetcar. They knew at once that they were made for one another despite the challenge of being too young and not sharing a common language. My mother was born in Vienna just at the outbreak of World War II. She met my father during the 1950s and fell in love.

My father was a GI stationed in Germany, protecting the western world from the impending Russian invasion. Not just a romantic star-crossed story of love that crosses language and culture, they've truly spent a nice life together. While they chose to move to America in the 1960s, one of the important aspects of European culture that my parents sought to share with me was an appreciation of aesthetics.

To take a difficult thing and make it simple for the moment, aesthetics is the philosophical study of the question: "What is beauty?" This is a challenging question that stirs up a discussion which touches on Gardner's Theory of Multiple Intelligences. After all, the whole impetus for Gardner's theory is to get away from the belief that intelligence is a single thing that, like beauty, can be defined in a single way. Commonly, many people resort to clichés in order to express a perspective on beauty. One of the great common clichés that we grow up hearing is, "I don't know how to explain beauty, but I'll know it when I see it".

It is interesting that so many of us automatically use the visual sense in order to define beauty. Before deciding anything else about something new, we first fix our eyes on it and decide if it is pleasurable. Gardner pointed out that our visual-spatial intelligence is a powerful tool that we use to organize our world.

Moving back in time, my youth was fairly typical. I went to school and struggled to follow along with the boring textbooks and the teachers who may or may not have had expertise in their areas of instruction. I remember a lot of worksheets and a lot of rote exercises. The teachers decided early on that I was not gifted and therefore only paid attention to me when I, in their eyes, misbehaved. I never really connected with the schooling, despite being constantly told that these classes would define my success in the future.

While I have fond memories of rainy winter days when my mother would drop me off in front of the state library free to roam through books full of stories that brought history and mystery to light, I lived, as so many of our young generations do, for summer vacation.

Summer vacation beckoned adventure. It meant that my family would be free to travel. My parents would scrape money together starting at about the end of my 8th grade year in order to travel to Europe or some other exotic destination. We never went out to dinner or movies; we couldn't be bothered. The money was set aside for more important things. We would visit different places each year and stay for weeks on end. Most of our trips were at least 5 weeks long. For our first trip, we traveled to Germany, Austria, and Switzerland in order to visit family. I was offered the opportunity to meet family about whom I'd only heard stories and seen in old faded and stained photographs.

Another year, we traveled to England. There, we explored London with all of its interesting nooks and culture. After getting used to driving on the other side of the road, though, we drove much farther afield. This was my first opportunity to experience Stonehenge. Even to my young and ill-informed sensibilities, Stonehenge was far more than a bunch of rocks stacked in a field in the middle of nowhere. In fact, I felt then and every time since then when I've visited, that, while there, I'm in the center of everything. After soaking in this esoteric place, we took off to Cornwall, the southern tip of England, to enjoy a week or two in a small miner's house on top of the red tin-filled cliffs dropping down into an icy and stormy grey ocean.

The hut was hundreds of years old and situated in the middle of potato fields. After the harvest, I took great joy in digging out the smaller potatoes left behind, filling my hands and shirt, and bringing the tubers home to form the center of a hearty stew. The cooking made the hut warm with a closeness that just isn't experienced in our modern dry-walled homes. Perhaps this warmth emanated from the walls which were made of giant boulders that had been plastered together.

The miner's hut was complete in all detail. It even featured a thatched roof that gave the place a dank smell during the rain squalls that constantly cruised off the ocean. I wonder if the giant rock walls, the thatched roof, and the raging fires beating back the cold ocean wind were visual cues that tied my experience together with a thread that comes partially from my imagination and partially from the deep history surrounding the place.

There, in Cornwall, we spent hours traveling down country lanes looking for ancient Celtic crosses that were left behind by the early population of Britain. I spent the weeks there cruising around ruins of great castles. Some of them are even reputed to be left behind by the real King Arthur, though nothing more than some vague outlines of walls can be seen. Here were piles of rocks that had once represented the great power of man in the world. The visual experience was unmistakable.

While nothing that I do will ever be permanent, stories and the knowledge contained by them are the closest that I will ever come to leaving a true and lasting mark on this world. Perhaps it was during this trip that I made my first vision to one day write a book.

During a different trip to Europe, my parents decided on France, which was a big favorite for them. We decided to travel through the Loire castles. These are a series of castles that line the countryside not too far from Paris. When I say castles, these do not conjure up the same visions of four giant walls and the towers that rise above for security in the truly medieval sense. Cannons had already become common; the time of big thick walls that could keep a battering ram at bay was already over by the time these beautiful palaces were built. They were built in the sixteen and seventeen hundreds for the French aristocracy notorious for their political and social intrigue.

While all of these chateaus were once the private retreats of the aristocracy, an escape from Versailles, they now welcome visitors onto their grounds complete with gardens, gift shops, and guided tours.

We spent our days strolling around the carefully manicured gardens and room after room of carefully crafted treasures. There were lily-covered ponds with swans. We saw priceless paintings, hand-carved wood beds, carefully chiseled fireplaces with finely detailed bas-relief that detailed the concerns of the people living there at the time. We stumbled through secret passages designed for all kinds of dirty deeds while hearing stories of intrigue and infidelity.

On our tours, we would often come to locked doors with a sign marked, "Private." Many of these castles are still the residences of the families for whom they were built. It must be fascinating for the children who grow up in places so filled with visually stimulating reminders of a rich history and a dark past.

Europe is filled with reminders of the power of religion. The once giant cathedrals that grace the bigger towns and cities of Europe fill their metaphysical purpose even now that they are dwarfed by more immediately powerful architecture. While the skyscrapers surrounding these cathedrals defy gravity and reflect the sky, these ancient Romanesque and gothic cathedrals still stir awe in the hearts of all who take the time to observe the detail that graces the fading and dirty artifices of these monuments to the religious-spiritual impulse that resides in each of us.

On the outside, there are images of saints rising into heaven and sinners being dragged to hell by demonic figures. There are gargoyles hanging from the rain gutters that would've struck terror into even the manliest man when caught out of the corner of an eye during the long and quiet twilight of a summer evening.

When standing inside the cold, dank, and dark interior of these old cathedrals, a full 10 degrees cooler than the outside temperature, the light filters through the stained glass stories reminding the visitor of the human struggle to focus on a spiritual path. The stained glass windows stretch all the way to the roof, as if to heaven. The amount of detail that was demanded in the design must have been a challenge for all of the artisans that worked to assemble them. Inside of the experience, an unmistakable lesson is being filtered into the eyes without a word needing to be spoken.

These windows withstand the endless years of human folly as if to tell anyone carefully looking that illumination cannot be experienced directly. Inside the most holy space, light has to come through the glass in order to reach the eyes. It's almost as if the builders were saying that God's message had to be filtered through the church's interpretation in order to be perceivable by man. This message has been under siege and in ever shrinking dominion ever since the reawakening of the Renaissance and the Age of Enlightenment. With the rediscovery of Greek and Roman thought and the mathematical achievement of the Muslim world, western European man would never be the same.

I've been blessed to spend days standing in front of Picasso's, Van Gogh's, and DaVinci's masterful artwork. The attention to the visual sense is phenomenal among the European arts. The Louvre, the Georg Pompidou Center, and the Musée d'Orsay are all filled with art work, but can also be considered artwork in their own right. The Louvre is a giant palace that was redesigned to hold some of the greatest treasures of our world. Wandering from room to room, one never knows whether an ancient Greek statue, a medieval tapestry, or an Egyptian talisman will find its way into one's gaze. From Abyssinian statues of Gilgamesh to DaVinci's Mona Lisa, the Louvre is a monument to the various expressions of visual representation for the last three thousand years.

In order to try to tie together the visual connection of three thousand years of history in the Louvre, a giant glass pyramid was built in the courtyard. With so much history held in a single place, it is fitting that an artist designed a meta-symbol that is both symbolic of what lies within as well as being a postmodern representation of one of the most ancient visual monuments in human society.

The pyramid clearly expresses the awe of early civilizations' architecture. In many areas of the world, our oldest civilizations have left behind strange structures that are, in many cases, some variation on the pyramid. At the same time as communicating something ancient, the glass, which is symbolic of ultra modern skyscrapers, that was used in its construction says that this is clearly a modern expression. This is a pyramid that does not bridge this world with the afterlife so much as it bridges the ancient world with the modern. It is because of this that some critics have called it a garish reminder of modern human being's lack of respect for the past. Regardless, the visual impact is immediate and lasting. One cannot walk away from the Louvre and not remember this giant pyramid in the courtyard.

The Musée d'Orsay, on the other hand, is a relic. It is a converted train station that revels in the art deco of the late eighteen and early nineteen hundreds. No effort is made on the outside to make it look anything other than what it is: a giant functional structure designed to assist travelers to find their way from point A to point B. It is crowned with a roof of glass allowing the natural light of the day to enter into the building. It is said that this naturally diffused light creates a viewing experience that is sublime when compared to the focus of common electric light. Inside, the art speaks the same language as the architecture of the building.

The museum is basically a giant room that has been divided with partial walls adorned with paintings that are cycled in and out from a massive collection of the famous Impressionist movement of the late eighteen hundreds. The Impressionist's art tries to capture a moment on a canvas. Instead of trying to communicate detail or symbolic meaning, the Impressionists worked hard to present the fleeting moment with an eye for truth. Just as our combination of intelligence is an intensely personal reality for each of us, so the Impressionist's art announces that we all see the world differently.

Despite the fact that a painting takes time to complete, these painters tried to snapshot a moment and communicate more than the visual elements. Laboring for hours over technique, they honed a craft that was startlingly different from the art that came before them. They tried, in their visual representation, to share with the viewer a feeling of the moment. The artists were clear that emotion is a key ingredient in the experience of the moment and that it, furthermore, could be depicted visually. While their art could be considered sloppy from one perspective, in that the techniques they used tried to speed the delivery of the paint to the canvas, one cannot deny the emotional content caught in the blobs of paint. These were artists who realized that the world was changing. They knew that they must evolve faster than ever in order to keep up with it.

This is healthy for us, though. We like to see the things that challenge us. It's important for us to externalize the deep-seated stuff that works within each of us.

In school, we love it when a teacher hands us a graph or a picture that helps us to understand a difficult concept for exactly this reason. We hate confusion. The visual aid helps minimize the gnawing feeling that maybe we, as students, just aren't smart enough to understand the concept being taught.

As a teacher, I love to work a white board with multiple colored pens. I try to use the pens consistent with the content I am presenting. For example, if I'm teaching grammar, then I will use the same color of pen to notate my subjects, predicate verbs, and a direct object or predicate adjective if present, in order to clearly show the students that, when found together, these parts are all segments of the independent clause. I make sure to use a different color to locate each of the various dependent clauses that make up our language. This helps the students to clearly and quickly see the differences between each of the clauses. Once the differences are visually cued, then the relationships become clearer.

I didn't always do this. I stumbled on it by accident one day and realized right away that the students seemed to be grabbing the information much more confidently than they had just minutes before. While it was a little more challenging for me, as I had to stay mindful of what each color represented, the payoff for the students was worth the extra attention.

Another real application of our visual intelligence becomes conscious in moments of conflict. When we get into a conflict, many of us want to have a moment on our own to reflect on what has happened. On top of this impulse, we may feel the need to picture what has happened. After all, if we can picture the moment which has developed a conflict, then we can better find a way to navigate into the future. We do tend to replay, like a looped film, challenging moments in our minds over and over. This is a natural way for us to explore what has happened so that we might glean more experience from the situation in order to handle a future situation with some similarities in a more successful manner. A very important kind of learning is our ability to picture a situation and visualize what has happened in order to develop better outcomes.

But our use of the visual intelligence isn't always so serious. I'm known for doodling when chatting on the phone or sitting in class, although I have always hated taking notes during the long-winded lectures of my professors. In fact, I hate to admit it, but I very rarely took notes throughout my education. So, I drew pictures. Let me be clear: I'm no artist. When it comes to drawing, even my stick figures look pretty lame. At the same time, I deeply enjoy just drawing lines and squiggles while I am on the phone or needing to listen to someone talk. Doodling helps me to focus on the ideas being presented. I feel an experience that can only be described as a heightening of my analytical skills.

Unfortunately, I also feel bad about this doodling habit. I remember that the teachers throughout primary and secondary school all told me that I was fooling around when scribbling doodles all over my notes.

Ironically, the doodles created more opportunity for my learning than the informational notes that I wrote. I didn't ever read my notes, after all. I much preferred reading the books about the subject matter. The textbooks usually felt rushed and one dimensional. So, the trips to the library did wonders to satisfy my curiosity in a way that my teachers could never understand. Clearly, this is a link to another of Gardner's described intelligences, the linguistic intelligence. The central point, though, remains the same: I had a method that helped my brain stay engaged.

Using these squiggles and doodles, I was able to keep my brain focused for longer and in a sharper way. At the same time, I was always getting into trouble for it. Rarely would a day go by without my name on the board with a check or two due to my fooling around. It's a shame that I became a discipline problem just because of a lack of understanding on the part of the teachers concerning my needs. Thankfully, I stayed true to my lack of interest in writing notes and have succeeded despite being told by a high school college counselor that I was not college material.

My success in college came from a persistence and curiosity that this world is filled with so many beautiful things and ideas. Close to my heart is the idea that, even if our human world is full of horror, disappointment, and confusion, we need to continue to challenge our consciousness to rise to new heights. It is only by developing our hearts and minds, in all of their inherent capacities, that we will close this loop. The great Isaac Asimov talked about this at great length. It is without a doubt that we can all see the truth that we will, to paraphrase him, never solve problems with the same level of thinking that created the problems in the first place. Of course we will, at the close of this loop, find ourselves deeply involved in a new world with new challenges.

"Linguistic intelligence involves sensitivity to spoken and written language, the ability to learn languages, and the capacity to use language to accomplish certain goals"

~ Howard Gardner

Chapter 7

Linguistic Intelligence
Verbal Exchange

When I think about the classic elements that constitute a stereotypical educational experience, I reflect on lectures, which included listening, note taking, and reading material that is the basis for, and supplemental to, the great and all-powerful professor's lecture. I don't mean this facetiously either. Almost all of my finest educational interactions occurred while I sat "at the feet" of these individuals who had invested so much of their life in the pursuit of knowledge.

When a student is truly interested in the subject, the time that we have with a true and recognized master of the field is filled with profound realization. Often, the feelings we experience during our direct interactions with these experts in the field help us to define a commitment for our own academic journey.

This classic transmission-style of academic content is an expression of our Linguistic intelligence. So much of our system of sharing specific and pointed knowledge challenges us to use this intelligence. In many ways, I agree with the classic perspective and feel that this intelligence is a crowning achievement of the human experience. However, saying that this crowning achievement, this capacity for language and for using it to share ideas and information, should be also recognized as the sole measurement of a human being's capacity to learn is problematic. Yet, because our education system focuses on this intelligence through deeply ingrained biases, this is exactly what happens.

Students with less maturity, who don't consciously or unconsciously understand the importance in pursuing a fluency in linguistic intelligence, get the message very quickly that they are probably not smart, not good students, and most assuredly not college material.

In fact, I recognize a very deliberate trajectory that moved me, as a student, away from a diverse approach to learning to one very focused on linguistic-based styles throughout my development. As I moved through high school, college, and university, I was expected to continually become more familiar and more comfortable in this dynamic. Continually developing my sensitivity for language was essential to my success.

During the early years in Elementary school, writing notes was required. My lack of willingness to write down the long boring lessons became a very traumatic experience for me. Because of my lack of interest in writing notes, I was forced to attend the dreaded parent-teacher meetings during which I would be berated for my blatant disrespect for the teacher's authority. Formalized action plans were always drawn up that ended with special accommodations that would earn me the insults of my peers. Often, I had to stop and show my notes to my teachers who would check them at the door before I could leave, and then made my parents sign these poor excuses for notes to prove that they had seen them.

I don't know if this is a common occurrence or just some special torture that was specially concocted just for me. Whatever the reality, I quickly became passive-aggressive about it: I would only write whatever the teacher had first written on the board, just so I wouldn't get in trouble.

The whole concept of writing notes escapes me even to this day. I didn't know what else to write aside from whatever the teacher first wrote. This behavior wasn't conscious, but I'd like to believe that if the teacher wasn't willing to write something on the board, then I shouldn't have to either. Granted, this attitude of mine may simply be a lingering bad attitude about the whole situation.

Later, as I reached the first stinky wisps of puberty, my lack of interest in note taking received threats of punishment. Scribbling every awful word from the teacher's mouth, whether in long-hand, shorthand, or in cursive, was something I just wasn't comfortable with doing; so, I spent many an afternoon copying from the dictionary while sitting in detention. I'm sure that I copied the entire dictionary at least once during these endless week after week afternoon detention marathons. Make no mistake: I wasn't a bad child. I never harmed anyone or made any problems that spelled out deep-seated emotional turmoil. I just didn't want to write notes.

Unfortunately, the teachers saw this as a challenge to their authority. After all, a child seemingly uninterested in absorbing all of the important messages and ostensibly proving it to anyone within eye-shot with a set of illegible chicken-scratch scribbles in a notebook, in the mind of the instructor, simply must not be absorbing anything.

How odd it is that, at home, my parents worried that I was too quiet and passive. The messages were clearly at odds. My parent's data simply didn't correlate with the comments made by teachers during parent-teacher conferences. The messages at school made me out to be some kind of obstinate monster. I was lucky that my parents were professionals: my father was a psychologist and my mother was a professor. They weren't too quick at believing that which they were told by these well-meaning instructors. I learned from all of this that there is a big space between how we learn and how we are taught.

As a young instructor, I fell quickly into the use of linguistic methods in my teaching. I love the give and take that comes with a verbal classroom. Wonderful energy ignites between teachers and students when everyone walks into a classroom excited to see one another and genuinely interested in participating in what could become one of their peak experiences in life. It makes the environment feel alive, crackling, dynamic. Once a class comes together and focuses on a topic, there is this feeling that something bigger than all the participants is happening. When the stage is set, all it takes to make this happen is a well-placed question.

The question is everything. It is the beginning and the end. The question is the hinge on which linguistic learning swings. The question swings the passive listener or reader into an active participant in learning.

The question cannot be forced. It is not an insidious thing that is furtively scribbled in a notebook during a late-night coffee binge. The well-designed question cannot be planned for. It is a creature born in the moment as the teacher interacts with the student. Furthermore, the question cannot be owned. It may come from the teacher or the student. Even more challenging, sometimes the question is asked by the professor to him or herself and sometimes it is asked by the student to him or herself. Most often, though, the questions sizzle across the classroom between the professor and the students, back and forth, building the energy and the excitement for the moment and the learning which is engendered by it. The question is an artifact emerging from the relationship between the teacher and the students.

Sometimes, this plays out in the most ridiculous and mundane situations. I remember one moment at the small private college in Honolulu where I taught English grammar for almost a decade.

Often, to get everyone's brain satisfactorily lubricated in order to present the day's lesson, I would start class with a formative assessment. Formative assessment is teacher-speak for an informal way to get a peek at the knowledge base within a student group. Using formative assessment, I try to see how flexible the intellectual content of the class is within the students' minds. It's great as it can be done with a quick question-answer dynamic that sets the tone of the class for new learning.

On one particular morning, I was working through my various questions asking about subjects, predicate verbs, and direct objects/predicate adjectives. I turned to a quiet student and asked, "Michelle, would you please give the class an example of a simple independent clause?"

"She walks."

"Thank you, Michelle, that was great. Chris, please tell me, what was this example's subject?"

"She."

"Nice! Good job, Chris. Tim, tell me, what was the predicate verb?"

"Walks."

"O.K., I think we're getting our rhythm. Let's keep this flowing..." I looked around for a student that was still not engaged. My eyes narrowed on Rosanne, "Rosanne, would you please give me an example of an independent clause with a direct object?"

There was silence for almost a minute. She thought I would give up and move on and ask the next person to assist, but I was in no rush this morning. I really wanted to know if she was learning. This young lady was hard to read and I had not been able to get a solid idea concerning where she was at. Finally, she straightened her arms and spoke. "I hate this fucking class!" she said loudly.

The class exhaled, wondering if there was going to be pain raining down. Instantly, everyone focused on the situation. They wanted to know how I would respond. For that matter, I wanted to know how I would respond. I had no idea. For a second, my mind raced: *Should I kick Rosanne out of class? Should I give her a tongue lashing in return for the nastiness that had just flown out of her mouth? Should I ignore the whole thing and just move on?*

No, I couldn't move on. I didn't want to fight with her. Kicking her out of class would have just handed her off to another person and would've solved nothing. In fact, there's a high probability that she said this in order to leave the room and escape the reality that she just hadn't learned the independent clause. None of these were solid solutions to either her remark or her clearly defiant attitude. I needed to send her a clear message that I cared for her learning, that I wasn't going to just push her through the class, and that this moment could be a pivot point for her entire future.

I took a deep breath and said, "Wow, Rosanne! This is an excellent, not to mention super, visceral, example of an independent clause with a dependent clause. Let's write it on the board and examine how it fits, with the class assisting us in identifying the grammatical pieces: The subject, predicate verb, and direct object. Let's see, Jenny, what was Rosanne's subject in this example?"

"I."

"Excellent! Now, James, what is the predicate verb here?"

"Hate."

"Nice job, James! That's a pretty strong predicate verb, isn't it?"

"Yes, Mr. O, it is a pretty strong word."

"So, Kim, what's a direct object again?"

"It's a noun right after the predicate verb, Mr. O."

"Right, so, what's the direct object in Rosanne's example, John?"

"Do I have to say the whole thing, Mister?"

"Do you feel uncomfortable repeating Rosanne's direct object, John?"

"Actually, I'm okay with it as long as I won't get in trouble."

"Then, go for it, John."

"'This fucking class' is Rosanne's direct object."

The class twittered. They knew they were witnessing something in this moment that was special. It wasn't special because, all of a sudden, nasty vocabulary words were flying around the classroom, although I'm sure that the language caught their scatological funny bones in just the right way. I'm sure they all thought that Rosanne, not a small or weak creature, was going to walk up to me after class and bust my lip for making a fool out of her. I certainly felt a laser stare burning into me for a while after this encounter. But, I didn't let it hold me back. I didn't stop the formative assessment dynamic just yet.

Of course, with the profanity written in bold markers across a white board, it was only a matter of time before a brave soul stuck his or her hand up and asked, "Why is that word considered bad?

Why does everyone make such a big deal out of it?"

This is a perfect example of the kind of moment when a student can ask a question that turns a whole class inside out and redirects it in a profound manner.

Laughing at the timing of his question, I told him that this was an excellent question that deserved a careful answer. Furthermore, I told him that I would answer this question as soon as we got a grip on our compound forms. Of course, everyone was absolutely intrigued by the whole situation. This group of students studied at light speed that day working to understand how to double and triple each of the parts of an independent clause: the subject, predicate verb, and direct object or predicate adjective, while keeping an eye on the clock to make sure that we found ourselves with enough time to address that cogent question still lurking "in the parking lot."

"The parking lot" was where we let unanswered questions sit before we had time to address them, especially if the question wasn't exactly focused on the material necessary for that lesson.

And so I swung for the fences on this one and began to tell the historical story about the moment our modern English began to evolve. I described the Anglo-Saxon world in England. We talked about how early English is primarily based on German, as the Angles and Saxons were Germanic tribes that had emigrated to Britain at various times over thousands of years of pre-historic human interaction. I told the students about the Battle of Hastings in 1066 AD when the Normans invaded England. I made sure to point out that the Normans were a group of people that came from what we would call France in our modern world. I took great pleasure in sharing with them that these people, these conquerors, spoke French as their native language.

We talked about the horrors of war. Rape, pillage, and enslavement were just a few of the defining features of war that were especially prevalent at that time. The students began to draw conclusions about what happened as the Normans established their control over their new land. Of course, it was pretty obvious that all of the people originally from England at this time had to quickly accept their fate and keep their heads down. They were no longer owners of their own culture; they were slaves to a new aesthetic, a concept or idea of what is good and beautiful.

It's important to make connections like this as ideas such as linguistic intelligence are explored. After all, languages each have ways of saying things that cannot be translated or shared in another language, except through translations that may suck all of the humor, playfulness, and life out of the ideas attempting to be conveyed. I once watched a classic American comedy film in Korea during which each Korean movie buff made dismissive grunting noises, got up, and huffed out of the theater until I was left all alone.

A famous baby-formula producer once designed packaging which was poorly translated into an African language and culture. African people often put pictures of the food ingredients on the packaging to ensure that the product is marketable among many language groups. Unfortunately, this manufacturer chose to place a picture of a beautiful baby on the packaging. Needless to say, not a single African chose the product as these people had zero interest in eating babies. The company lost millions upon millions of dollars because of the nuance of language and culture.

Sometimes, even more insidiously, the original meanings of words can be subverted, turned into dark and sinister vocabulary, something dirty because of the political implications that come

Falling but Fulfilled

along with war and the cultural blitzkrieg that often follows closely in violence's wake. After 1066, the people who originally owned English lost their exclusive rights to it. The language that we speak in our modern times still carries these politics.

Consider the word "cunning." The word is an adjective. Originally, it was used specifically to describe the female intelligence. This adjective was taken from a noun that cannot be written without receiving total hatred from women everywhere. Drop the "–ing" and add a "t." Here is a perfect example of the damage of 1066. To this point, the word that shall not be written was the proper Anglo word to name that part of the body which brings new life into this world. How can that be a dirty word? My students were stunned silent.

Then, one of them asked, "Well, what about the word vagina?"

"What about it? It comes from a French word. That's right. And, you should know that the word shit and piss is much the same, as well. Each of these has an exact synonym to talk with in a proper manner, as in to a doctor."

They were stunned as I listed the official French words, many of which have derivatives in modern English that have become our acceptable words to talk about bodily functions in a polite manner. We say that these words: urinate, excrement, and intercourse—derived from coitus—are acceptable. These words mean the same as piss, shit, and fuck, but haven't given children soap-washed mouths for nearly a millennium.

There's only one really good satisfying conclusion to be made: the politics of 1066 are still hanging around. Even in our challenging and open-minded worlds, so many of us are completely unaware of how our past affects our future. And as for this little story about the origin of bad words, while linguists everywhere may be laughing at my profoundly incorrect assumptions, I cannot think of an easier and more elegant manner in which to show that our language is tricky and can teach us ideas and beliefs just by speaking about them.

Of course, the students were quick to ask the next question, "Well, Mister, if the English were defeated by the French at the Battle of Hastings and watched their world get terminated along with their language turned into the nasty and harsh sound of the dirty pig farmers and chamber pot cleaners, then why do we say, 'Excuse my French,' every time we curse?"

I answered him succinctly, "That's what we call irony."

"Logical-mathematical intelligence involves the capacity to analyze problems logically, carry out mathematical operations, and investigate issues scientifically"

~ Howard Gardner

Zachary M. Oliver

Chapter 8

Logical-Mathematical Intelligence
Finding Meaning in Numbers

In our modern world, our society seems to have developed a very strong bias towards the idea that analytical thinking is the highest form of all possible thought. Tests purporting to measure human intelligence, such as the IQ test, look primarily at our ability to process data using rigid and formulaic channels of thought at very deep levels in order to measure our intelligence. The expectation is that we, if we are really smart, should be able to think through a variety of data using the same basic analytic tools and apply them sequentially to break down complex problems into simpler forms.

This is the essential nature of mathematics, a sort of consciously developed academic language that operates in a purely analytical manner. Gardner discusses this kind of intelligence in his theory and labels it Logical/Mathematical Intelligence.

In applying this style of thinking to our education system, we can recognize that, to a large degree, our entrance into college is based on the Scholastic Aptitude Test (S.A.T.), which is based on the same kinds of content as the IQ test. The S.A.T. is a massive source of stress for teenagers as it marks a rite of passage into adulthood. I relate to the trauma of this rite of passage and the absolute confusion it can create in the futures of droves of students. As I was preparing to write my doctoral dissertation, this trauma was an excellent point to begin my sifting of the complex situation.

While I wasn't sure where this line of reasoning would take me, I chose to dedicate considerable time over the course of a couple of years using my Logical/Mathematical Intelligence to break apart and simplify my thinking into categories or themes that would eventually allow me to find a researchable topic.

My reflection on my own experience was a great and personal place to start. It occurred to me that our society has its own right of passage from youth into adulthood that offered some wisdom as to what our world values as intelligence. I began to think of the S.A.T. scores as a kind of statement both coming from us, as new adults, to society, as well as a statement from society concerning how our performance thus far in life might be evaluated.

For some of us, this test may be the first time that we feel the adult world breathing down our neck. The S.A.T. score can be a "Screw You" for those who didn't try, scored a 900, and are not motivated to attend college; it can be an informal ranking among interested college-bound friends; and/or the score can be, as it was in my case, a tragic limiter of options.

In thinking about the statement society makes to us about our performance, the message is fairly clear. Our access to affordable public education is, in some way, limited for those among us who have *not* developed the kind of thinking that is evidenced on the kinds of tests that measure analytic ability. However, what happens to a late bloomer?

I have no doubt that there is some research that shows a correlation between age and analytical thinking skills. While the

IQ test does factor in age, the S.A.T. doesn't. It simply scores correct answers across a set of questions that are virtually the same for all graduating seniors. I remember taking it over and over in preparation for my entrance into college. Unfortunately, despite my sort-of respectable showing of a 1200 score, I was denied access to any of the California system public universities as an incoming freshman.

Very specific and formally defined scores are needed in order for applicants to access the various tiers of schools available for these would-be incoming freshmen. The tiered system of matching scores to access for college education smacks of a modern day caste system. It isn't as if any student can decide to attend a Harvard or a Princeton. These students need to have the evidence that backs their application, the kind of evidence that is typically presented through scores on these huge standardized tests. And I just didn't score high enough to beat out the multitude of high school seniors preparing their own college applications. Despite having led an interesting life full of varied and rich experience, my 1200 labeled me as someone who was simply not, in the words of my college counselor, "college material".

While it is understandable that, because big public money is spent assisting students through their education, the government wants to ensure that they are investing in students with the best possible chance for success, many students are being left behind just because they can't evidence the same thinking process which is most successfully measured by the S.A.T.

Even then, the attempt to measure intelligence and then financially support those individuals who have it hasn't exactly been a winning strategy. I believe that this is what led to my being labeled as not someone who was worth the investment as an incoming college freshman. Instead, I was left to my own devises to figure out an alternate route to pursue an education or get swallowed by the thousand distractions that litter a teenager's life.

While I was accepted to some expensive and small private liberal arts universities, the tuition and living costs of these schools were prohibitive. I was not eligible for the financial aid and my parents were not able to bear that kind of additional expense. I was forced to attend community college and stay close to home in preparation for an opportunity to transfer into the public university system as a junior.

Unfortunately, community colleges are not much more successful at moving students through to completion than the big public universities that they seek to support. Looking back, I was being prepared for rejection. Of all of the people I attended class with and stayed in contact with through the years, very few moved on to graduate from university. We had to fight through little to no university-transfer advising, big anonymous classes, and careless instruction with little student-instructor interaction in order to even be considered for a shot at my eventual destination, the University of California, Berkeley, which was characterized by the same exact kind of careless and disinterested academic environment.

This traditional education system has been cracking for years, perhaps for an entire generation. In fact, I would even venture a guess that the entire movement towards more and more for-profit education institutions is a direct response to exactly these kinds of problems. While these for-profit schools tend to be expensive, they are still attractive in that they are designed specifically around the student experience, especially the prospect of online learning and all of the freedom of time that makes it so attractive to non-traditional students who are typically adults with families and careers. Online classes offer assignments that can be done in the middle of the night or during lunch breaks. These schools offer large online databases that assist student research at times when libraries would typically be closed. The flexibility of these environments is a great strength.

These for-profit institutions aren't without their challenges, however. Currently, the for-profit education world, from an academic perspective, is thoroughly ensconced in what can best be described as a curriculum-centric perspective. This strategy comes from the business world's concept of quality assurance.

Curriculum, in the minds of those who are developing these systems, offers a unifying element across vast areas of space. Furthermore, if a curriculum can be standardized and implemented across a big network, then it can be easily managed, from an IT perspective, across the wide spectrum needed for a school operating in a virtual environment.

When a university is spread across a nation with many different campuses that have to offer basically the same education and the same product-experience, the most obvious and easiest method to communicate the university's programs is through a single curriculum. When considering the surge of attention given to the new models of online learning, which is not only spread across a vast distance but also across time, the concern is consistency. This need for consistency speaks directly to the drive for accreditation felt by these for-profit schools. Schools work hard to achieve benchmarks that allow them to apply for and advertise various levels of accreditation. These accreditations represent, for lack of a better word, legitimization.

This adaptation of the university into the Internet modality triggered me. After all, the ability for students to have access to a legitimate and accredited education without having any face to face obligation to a university creates mind-boggling opportunities from a business perspective. There are many potential students who when washed out of the public university track decided to begin their lives, instead of waiting around for an opportunity to attend school. This online modality offers these potential students an opportunity to reawaken their learning potential, to cultivate an understanding in a subject area that inspires them, and to eventually pursue the true career of their dreams. From a leadership perspective, it is easy to see that our current understanding of online education is simplistic at best and needs a lot of attention in order to be developed in deeply effective ways.

It was in this milieu that I discovered a potential dynamic area which I wanted to discuss during my graduate school work. Most importantly, as I reflected about this, I realized that I wanted to begin looking at this problem of online learning in a methodical manner. While I was never especially cognizant of my Logical/Mathematical Intelligence, I realized that an investigation into this challenging world would need carefully planned steps that would assist me to begin to formulate clearer thoughts about what really matters, namely how do students learn and what stands in their way of getting the education that is so necessary for a productive career in our new information and service-based economy.

My first attempt was a legitimate way to begin to address the question, "How do we learn?" in the smallest and most focused manner possible. I quickly abandoned this goal, though, as it seemed just too large, too intimidating.

As I began to look at the story of learning, I found that it is a far more complex story than I might ever have an opportunity to pursue. Without access to an M.R.I. and a fancy lab full of technology and assistants with potential research subjects lining around the block, this question about how humans learn was sadly just out of reach. In order to pursue this question, I would probably need to start collecting doctoral degrees in psychology, biology, chemistry, and linguistics, among others.

I had a unique opportunity at the time. Besides studying in a notable online school for a master degree in education with a focus on instructional technology, I was teaching grammar and writing at a small college which had gone to great length to train me as a coach of an online learning tool that they had invested in as the beginning of an exploration concerning how online education might be the wave of the future. So, I devised an experiment to find out if learning environments affected learning.

Research is a brave act. I don't think it usually gets recognition as this, but it takes deep faith to throw a belief out there into the world and find out if it really bears any truth. I wasn't sure if online learning environments would affect the learning of those individuals in my class who would be lucky enough to experience it, but I knew that someone had to ask the question and find out if there was anything, an important strand of questioning, to develop further.

I started with a question that looked something like: Do learning environments, online or face to face, have any significant affect on student performance? And, because researchers are forced to start research with a guess, I proposed that learning environments do affect student outcomes. At the time, I wasn't willing to guess how the environment in which a student learns would affect outcome, but I could feel the gears turning inside of me telling me that there must be some difference.

So, I offered my guess up for testing, to see if I could find my first slice of truth. This truth would be neither simple nor clear. And it would certainly not be definitive. In my mind, nothing about human subject research is ever definitive; there are simply too many variables at work every step along the way. Furthermore, in the words of my methodology mentor, Dr. Donna Duellberg, "No research instrument can ever be perfect."

To prepare for this experiment, which would become the focus of my master's thesis, I had a few things to think about. First of all, I wasn't going to be able to use a really varied sample of individuals to try to gather any evidence about whether or not learning online affects student performance. I was, after all, only teaching a couple of sections of the same content at a small private for-profit college in Honolulu. So I chose to do a little careful manipulation of the problem by grouping those students available to me into two equal groups. To form these groups, I gave my two sections of the same class a test that I knew would help me split the students equally according to their grammar ability.

Equality in performance among these two groups was a careful calculation on my part that allowed for me to get data that, while not perfect, could minimize questions that might come up about the experiment. I wanted to make sure that whatever I found had grounding in reality and wasn't some bizarre mistake that came out because of the small group of people participating in my research.

I knew that clear thinking in my design would allow for better and clearer conclusions, and so I spent many sleepless nights fussing over my design to make sure that both groups had access to the same information and the same access to answers for their individual questions.

Next, I met with each group separately and outlined the

instructions that would guide their studies during the next week and a half. One group was given an online orientation, while the other was told when and where to show up for class.

Of course, the students stuck in class were not happy that many of their friends had been excused. I did take a minute to record these reflections. The students expressed that they wanted to be given the flexibility to not be required to come to the class during the course of the experiment.

Without meaning to jump too far ahead, it was these observations that triggered a separate thought process on my part that led to my doctoral dissertation. It was clear that, given the option, students with no prior experience of online learning all clearly described that they would prefer not to have the time obligation of a face to face campus experience.

In many ways, this didn't surprise me. If an easier way to attend school with less restricted time commitment could be negotiated, then most students would readily jump at the opportunity. If I remember my life as a student correctly, I don't think that I would have chosen any differently. It was this reflection about selection of environment that I would return to for my doctoral research a few years later.

A week and a half later, all the students reconvened in my class and took their first test. Because I knew who was in each group—online or face to face traditional, it was easy for me to track the grades and develop an average score for each group. After collecting the tests, I again gave direction to the online group to attend online for another week and a half. I reminded them that they still had an obligation to log in and work through the online materials I had developed for them there. After working on some new concepts for the face to face traditional group, I released them and turned my attention to the tests and the data awaiting me.

This was the first of the big payoffs.

After tabulating the basic descriptive stats, such as mean, mode, and median, on a useful little spreadsheet, I found that the average score for both groups fell into the "B" range. Even though at first glance this looks like nothing, there were some major discrepancies between these two "B" range scores representing each group.

On the first assessment, the online students scored significantly better than the face to face traditional group. In fact, this group's average was much closer to an "A," while the face to face traditional group narrowly avoided scoring in the "C" range. I remember being stunned that the online group was so much more successful during the first part of the research.

During the next test, however, a very interesting shift occurred. This time there was no significant difference between the scores among each group. The online group basically produced a group average score that was the same on the second test as the first. Their performance, while showing strong improvement during the first week and a half period, flat-lined between the first and second filtering test. In contrast, the face to face traditional group, which had scored less well on the first filtering test, dramatically improved on the second exam. In fact, the group average was solid enough to push the group into the "A" range, narrowly passing the average of the online group. In the end, the traditional face to face group outperformed the online group despite the fact that the two groups were matched academically.

It's challenging to know exactly what happened to these students during the research. Of course, there are many problems with gathering information from tests. If I apply my analytical intelligence, then I can quickly point out that there are a number of uncontrollable influences on the students who were participating in this experiment. These are called, in the parlance of research, "confounding variables" because they may affect the data collected by the researcher in ways that cause a lack of clarity when interpreting the results.

Maybe some of the students worked the night before the test. Perhaps another had a fight with a boyfriend or girlfriend in the car on the way to school that morning. Traffic could've made another student late for school, maybe causing him or her to miss the opportunity to eat something. After all, stress and hypoglycemia must surely have some affect on a person's ability to think clearly, especially when it comes to something as mechanistic as grammatical structure.

What I do like about this research is that, however small it was, it did try to pursue whether there is a performance difference for students when they learn online versus when they attend a class. It seems that there was some evidence that there was a difference. While the end result was basically the same, the trajectory of results between these two groups showed a radically different path. A blended online-face to face atmosphere might make for another interesting experiment.

Fast forwarding to a present in which I work for a university that prides itself on its blended model, I can say that the blended model is like any other blend of anything: it is nothing more than a mélange of all of the best and worst elements of its antecedent parts.

Perhaps, using the results of this research, a case could be made for a learning environment that begins online and then transforms into a traditional learning experience as it progresses to its conclusion. In this way, students might experience the quick improvement that I found in the online group through the first exam. Then, for the second half of the class, perhaps as the students work to connect the material into long-term memory, the experience of working face to face with an instructor may be the most effective blend between both of these environments.

The problem is that I, as the researcher and as a university leader, don't know whether the quick improvement was because of the efficacy of the environment, the novelty of the environment, or by the fact that they were participating in research and therefore were more alert than usual.

Re-tooling my research perspective during my doctoral work, I began to sniff many of the confounding variable problems inherent to research of human beings with all of our beautiful complexity. Besides the challenging reality that we, as scientists, have yet to definitively describe how learning occurs biologically, we also can't begin to fathom all of the environmental influences that affect learning.

As I mentioned earlier, I decided to look more closely at the wish, so powerfully expressed by students, to be free from having to come to the campus every day. After all, as a maturing researcher, I was aware that asking people with experience in both environments about their impressions of each, while somewhat superficial, did allow me a picture into their preferences, as well as their perceptions concerning the respective successes and failures of each.

Harking back to the perspectives that my first online students had expressed upon conclusion of the research, I somehow expected that a group of students with experience in both online and face to face traditional learning environments would probably express some pretty strong preferences favoring one of the learning environments.

This was a huge challenge, though. I wasn't sure how to approach the problem of looking at perceptions and predilections for any particular learning environment. It's one thing to ask people about their perceptions about something; however, we can never be sure if there is anything reliable about the responses that are made. Different people can read the same question in very different ways.

The first task that I had to address in my design was to create something which I could use to collect participants' perspectives and predilections about online and face to face traditional learning environments. The Perception Inventory, as it became known, was based on a very simple kind of survey, called a Likert scale survey, which allows participants to report about their perspectives using simple responses that range from "strongly agree" to "strongly disagree." As I thought about the challenge of asking for people's opinions, I realized that there would have to be two halves of this survey so that participants would retain the ability to report any variation or no variation between their online and face to face traditional learning environment experience.

The plan for collecting the data needed for my dissertation was to first administer the Perception Inventory in order to record perspectives about learning environments before affecting the participants' self-perceptions through the introduction of multiple intelligences. As each participant took the MIDAS, it was important for me to coach each participant through the process of understanding Howard Gardner's theory and to interpret each participant's MIDAS on the spot, if they so wished.

While most of the students took the opportunity at that

moment to really dig deeply into the meta-cognitive evaluation that the MIDAS produced, others contacted me later with questions. While these conversations were really satisfying to me, as I was afforded the opportunity to provide a real and solid service to these students, it was not an integral part of my research. Those who were not interested in my help simply flashed their scores for me so that I could identify what each person's primary intelligence group was at that point in time.

You see, I wanted to see if people that share a primary invested-in intelligence would also share similar perceptions about both learning environments.

While the results were very interesting, they were not at all what I expected. When formulating my hypotheses, I expected to find that some of the primary intelligence groups would be pulled toward preferences to one or the other learning environment. What I found was that every group, in every instance, expressed perceptions that can only be described as an overarching preference for the face to face traditional environment over the online experience. This blew my mind. How is it that everyone in my sample who had taken classes both online and face to face preferred face to face classes in every single case?

In some instances, the differences were statistically significant between an intelligence group's average score on each half of the Perception Inventory comparing that group's online to face to face experience. In others, even though statistical significance could not be found, a simple glance at the averages show that, while the gap was narrow between the matched averages for both environments, the students expressed favorable perceptions in every situation of the face to face traditional learning environment.

To figure out all of this, I had to put my own intelligences through a kind of evolution. As I've previously written, I am not naturally a strong logical/mathematical learner. In fact, I tend to look at formal logic as a quaint tool that only defines a very narrow kind of thinking. In partnership with a whole lot of critical thinking, this logical/mathematical approach helped me to plan this research.

However, this thinking also had its limits. As I became conscious of my Logical/Mathematical Intelligence, I realized that I needed to repeatedly partner with my other intelligences throughout the conceptualization process as well as when the data started taking shape. I felt that I was constantly slipping in and out of the various intelligences as I navigated the real-world dynamics inherent to human subject research. This research was far more than a string of symbols on a page that I was crunching in order to break the complex forms into the easiest and most basic conceptual parts.

Gardner makes a careful discussion throughout his work that no attempt should be made to try to identify a single intelligence as superior to any other. He goes to great lengths to explain the importance for us to develop each of the intelligences in order for us to bring our thinking processes to full fruition. I can see that this was true for me as I pursued the final stage of my doctoral study, the much-feared dissertation. I was challenged to dig deeply into my various thinking processes, to create successful responses for the problems I was facing.

I spent a lot of time in introspection, reflecting on what I was looking for and what I might find. Music was a constant companion of mine and kept me in balance as I worked through elements I was less confident in, such as piling together the statistics I needed to complete my dissertation. My favorite way of paring away the unnecessary complexity in my research methodology was through the continual drawing and redrawing of a flow chart on big white boards to sharpen my mind's perspective about ways in which I might be wasting time and effort.

Obviously, this research could not have been done without some intense social interaction. Not only did I spend a lot of time interfacing with the participants of the research, I also worked hard to develop the social ties necessary for me to be welcomed into the institution which ended up hosting my endeavor. Also, it would be a lie if I were not to acknowledge the profound realizations that occurred as I sat behind a computer keyboard struggling to get my data clearly onto a page.

Finally, the long walks that I took with my wife and children that kept my body moving and enjoying the beautiful natural environment of Hawaii kept my life from becoming unhinged as my brain struggled with wrapping itself around some small challenge in the path of future students wishing to pursue an education on their terms and in their own ways. At that point in my almost purely academic focus, I struggled to maintain some kind of health through one of the most intense experiences of my life.

I flourished through this process, not because of my intense concentration on any single intelligence, but in the combination of all of them. If anything, this is the key lesson of my last decade of teaching and learning: Education is an intensely personal experience unique to each individual. Not only does most education occur just beyond the edges of a curriculum, but also it takes our persistence, our mindful attention, and a total inclusion of our efforts, both conscious and unconscious, to discover success and to not lose our balance as we pursue the most challenging among our goals.

Both the traditional and the for-profit universities have forgotten that, for successful education to occur, we need to become wholeheartedly committed to understanding our students, and learn to develop them using the raw materials that they are motivated by in order to succeed.

**

Questions such as these need to be asked: Can Multiple Intelligences Theory help people to determine if and why people naturally gravitate towards certain types of careers or career paths? If a group of learners are successful or unsuccessful in one kind of learning environment, then could/will these learners be successful in another? What qualities do these unsuccessful and successful learners share? How do these qualities correlate with the learning environment? What can an organization do to ensure that the vast amounts of money for training, whether in a for-profit, non-profit, or training investment capacity, will be spent in an effective manner? These are just a few of the basic questions that need more exploration and volumes of research. Of course, there will be no definitive answers.

The human animal is complex, varied, and deeply nuanced. At the same time, though, there are many universal qualities present across the spectrum of individuals. It is my hope that the universal qualities that arise out of our biological similarities can be described adequately for educators, researchers, and leaders to make the best decisions possible in advancing technological solutions that can work successfully for the greatest amount of people, while still recognizing and respecting all of the varied individuality that continually reinvigorates the beauty of human interaction, the relationships that develop from these interactions, and the communities that create such rich experiences for the individuals participating in them.

"But there is a revolution which is entirely different and which must take place if we are to emerge from the endless series of anxieties, conflicts, and frustrations in which we are caught. This revolution has to begin, not with theory and ideation, which eventually prove worthless, but with a radical transformation in the mind itself"

~ Jiddu Krishnamurti

Chapter 9

On Motivation

I arrived earlier than usual at Mr. Sun's office one late summer morning. Sitting in the dark conference room, I felt homesickness circling around me. By this time, I had already been in South Korea for many months and had grown accustomed to its energy and pace. I was, at this point, immersed in my life abroad.

At the same time, quiet moments, such as this one, in the pre-dawn among the ultra modern artwork shadowed in a dark Samsung conference room, brought up a lot of turmoil. This is the real curse for expatriate workers spending long periods investing time and energy in another country. Everything is fine when catapulting through the novel adventures in an exotic world. On the flipside, though, is an exhaustion that sneaks up during quiet moments. This weariness comes with the territory. Everyone knows about it, but it is certainly never included in the job description or contracts. Perhaps the promise of adventure quiets the reasonable mind in each of us that would typically warn us of living life in a strange world.

It must have been around September when I found myself sitting and waiting for Mr. Sun in the Samsung compound. I had already tasted a lot of adventure during my time in this country.

I had already visited the DMZ splitting North and South Korea. Standing at the war memorial, I remember shivering there in the quiet. Not a relaxing quiet, it was a thick and tense feeling that hung over that valley separating the two nations still laced together with machine gun emplacements, subterranean caves, and land mines.

Climbing to the top of Sorak-San, I had participated in a favorite Korean pastime of *soju*-fueled mountain climbing and *Kim Bap* munching.

I had visited the beaches of Kang Nung and had enjoyed the deep ocean salt water baths available in the town. In these baths, great expense is taken to pump the water into private clubs which allow bathers to enjoy the bracing cold water as part of a restorative therapy. My student guides told me, with a snicker, that it would be good for my manhood.

During a visit to a palace, I had even been dressed up as a traditional Korean groom and put into a festival that paired up couples. My students did this as a joke. Alas, none of the blushing brides chose this *Me Guk* teacher. I guess I just didn't quite look the part.

Sitting there in the dark at the Samsung compound, my mind focused alternately on the various memories of this experience in Korea and the pull of the surf back home at Diamond Head just off Waikiki. I was caught somewhere in between. The air was warm and wet this morning as was often the case during the summer months in Korea. I was looking forward to this lesson; I hadn't seen Mr. Sun for a couple of weeks. Due to the level of his position, he was required to travel from time to time. His trips to Russia, Japan, and Washington D.C. always sparked some very interesting discussions.

When the light snapped on, I sprung to my feet. While I had been working with Mr. Sun for many months, I certainly felt the seriousness implicit in my time with him and looked forward to the clarity and focus of our discussions. He laughed when he saw me sitting in the dark, turned to his newly-arrived assistant, and asked her to bring us coffee.

We usually drank tea, not coffee. He must've been tired that morning, as well. Stumbling from the conference room to his office, I stood quietly waiting, sheepishly, as he took a moment to move around the room, organize his belongings, and collect his thoughts. I was always self-conscious about sitting before being asked. This hesitancy was a little of my left-over old-world European breeding. I seized the moment to pick sleep from my eyes and work on the haze in my mind. After a moment, the coffee arrived. It smelled really welcoming on this morning.

Instead of sitting down in his big chair, the usual signal for me to sit as well, Mr. Sun waved to me to walk with him out onto the sun deck next to his office. As we stepped through the door, I could see the small red ball of the sun rising up through the early morning fog, clinging to the rice paddies that stretched out and climbed the hillsides starting just outside the gate of the Samsung compound. I remember finally understanding why the Japanese flag with its single red dot was chosen to represent the rising sun. I had never seen the sun like this. It was a beautiful morning and neither of us wanted to begin too quickly, so we sipped our coffee in silence.

Hearing a few whistles and calls from below, we stepped to the edge of the deck and looked at the sports field adjacent to the building. Below, a soccer game was just beginning to take shape. For a few more minutes, we watched as the players stretched their muscles and began to run around the track to warm up. A few minutes later, Mr. Sun turned to me and began a conversation that would stretch over the course of the next few months, surfacing each time with interesting new facets. It's a conversation that reverberates for me even now a full decade later which gave vocabulary to a way of thinking that had already begun to develop within me.

"How do we motivate people?"

At first, I didn't understand. Why would he ask such a question to a young English teacher?

"As an employer, you pay them," I said.

"Yes, I pay them…"

He was quiet for a few moments watching the kick-off to the game going on below us. I'm sure that he was putting himself into my shoes, a young man with little experience of leading people. Mr. Sun was a patient man. I'm sure this is why he was so well respected.

"Well then, what is the way we motivate people without money? Money is an unsatisfactory way to motivate because of human nature," he said.

"What about human nature?"

"People always want more than what they have. There is not enough money in the world to motivate someone to do something. This can only be a short-term solution. "

"I suppose that if money is ineffective then people will often be motivated by promotion," I said.

"Yes, promotion is another common idea. I shared this perspective too. I think that I'm moving away from it, however. It seems that this only works for some people some of the time. Others are not interested in promotion. How do I motivate them?"

"Are we speaking only of positive motivational tools, Mr. Sun, because fear can be a powerful motivation."

"I would prefer not to use fear; it also seems too common."

"You know, I've never really thought about this, Mr. Sun. It's not something that my liberal arts background focused on."

"Yet, here we are asking the question nonetheless. The challenge with this question is that no two people are truly the same. So no two motivational tools are the same. What works for one individual may or may not work for the next."

"This is true, Mr. Sun. Also, culture is the same way. We each have a lot of influence by our culture concerning what we find good or pleasing. In order to connect with this level of influence, many individuals have pursued art. After all, art seeks to reflect culture and indicate opportunities for growth or to point out mistakes or distortions in thinking. Art has always had a very subversive edge."

This was something that I had, luckily, a clue about.

"Yes...and so the question of motivating a person without money or fear is truly one worth a lot of effort. The interesting thing is that it cannot be controlled. We have begun thinking about some of the social challenges in our country. In an effort to change the thinking, we have been investing in a very long-term project. We have begun to pay for soap operas here in South Korea. They are very popular and can act as a guide for social change."

"Are you serious? How can you do this without being accused of controlling the media?"

"Aha," he said, "this is the question. Korea has a long history of controlling the media; this is not so difficult. The better question is: Why?"

"Because you want to try to engineer positive social change."

For a few minutes longer, we watched the soccer game, musing on the joys of kicking a ball around. The sun was no longer a little red ball hovering above the hillside. It had grown in intensity, much like our discussion, until it began to give off the late summer heat that causes the cement to shimmer.

This man was not just talking about manipulating characters and content in soap operas in order to affect change. He was talking about a form of education. With his colleagues, the vague "we" whom he referred to in our conversation, he was working on a way to set benchmarks for the growth of human consciousness. He had a goal for Korea that he felt poised to successfully engineer. Without wanting to sound like an alarmist, it scares me to even think about it. Finding a way to motivate people through the gift of a positive and fulfilling vision for the future is not a negative thing, in and of itself. Unfortunately, this kind of idea raises the specter of monsters like Hitler, who fervently worked to create a world forged from a vision of enhanced consciousness. It doesn't surprise me for a moment that Hitler was an artist, whether successful or not. He certainly lived in a carefully constructed aesthetic.

Engineered social change sounds a lot like education, just without the technical vocabulary that usually accompanies the formal field of study. Education shapes the individuals that move through it. It is the interpreter of culture. Education, in its purest theoretical discussions, is always underlined by the topic of aesthetics: What does a good society look like? Who participates in a good society? What does this individual need to know in a good society? What place does learning have in a good society? Or, does only training have a place in a good society? How does an individual in a good society think about knowledge?

This list of questions does not even begin to cover the scope of the discussion going on within the field of education. Reflecting on the common thread of power that weaves through these questions, I recognize how integral a role education plays in communicating what is important to a society and in enhancing or curbing the freedom its individuals have for the conscious ability to articulate their perspective, goals, and visions.

Mr. Sun and I circled around and touched on this topic many times over the course of the next few months. On one such occasion, he mentioned that his team already had computer chips in prototype form that were well beyond 10 times those that were commercially available at the time. Furthermore, he had just been able to mass produce these silicon chips. I remember that this amazed me; I couldn't imagine why his company hadn't aggressively released these to the public.

Mr. Sun was, as always, very patient with my impetuousness. He explained that while his team was able to produce this technology which was far ahead of the industry standard, the computer programmers responsible for designing programs that could use this technology were nowhere close to being ready.

Dumbfounded, I listened as he told me that the programmers needed time to grow the capacity to dream what might be the potential for the technology. The human element and imagination had yet to catch the cutting edge. This blew my mind as I had always been steeped in a tradition of liberal arts which gave the message that, when the mind is ready, the technique will appear. Here, the chip was ready, but the technique was not.

Connecting the dots back to the conversation concerning the influence on Korean soap operas, I realize a similar message was being presented. The Korean people, deeply involved with their televisions, needed an aesthetic to work toward which has the capacity to challenge the growth of consciousness. Beyond the intense work ethic prevalent throughout the society, these people spend a lot of time soaking up the stories of these soap operas. The characters and plot lines generate much conversation throughout the long days of work and play.

Whether working at home or among the millions of small businesses, the stories permeated throughout society like a new mythology assisting the people by forcing them to take a look at the bad habits which have held their society back and by giving them forward-thinking characters ready to move Korean society into the 21st century. Mr. Sun and his group of like-minded compatriots had already developed the idea of a futuristic Korean society and were trying to assist the common Korean people in shaping the dream of what to do with this future.

At the time, I knew this was a watershed moment in my development. I was both young enough to be simply in awe of what I was having the opportunity to peer into, as well as scared of the power that permeates from a perspective such as Mr. Sun's.

I can recognize the brilliance, the absolute clarity of vision, inherent to Mr. Sun's plan for the development of his culture. I even agree with the content of this dream. I agree with the importance of raising consciousness among our fellow human beings. At the same time, I, as an educator and as a social scientist, want nothing to do with crafting the end product of my instructional moments. I disagree with those in my field that believe that outcomes, or as we call them, learning outcomes, can and/or should be quantified.

As investigated by the noble field called the philosophy of science, the danger is this: we never know the repercussions of our actions when we begin to manipulate and control the many aspects and elements of our universe.

Equipped with a whole new perspective and purpose of life, I began to prepare myself for the time when I would return to my own homeland. My return would be, I resolved, much different than my departure. I was no longer lost and without aim. My career was beginning to form around a mission that I could taste. By creating opportunities for exciting educational moments among a community of learners, the lessons I had learned through my experiences in Korea and through my discussions with Mr. Sun would manifest in Hawaii with people who shared so many values and moments. Like Mr. Sun, I wanted to lay the groundwork for culture and consciousness building. I knew this was a worthwhile goal to dedicate my life to and continue to stand by that decision even now, a decade later.

"That we each have a unique blend of intelligences leads us to the most important implication of the theory for the next millennium. We can choose to ignore this uniqueness, strive to minimize it, or revel in it"

~ Howard Gardner

Chapter 10

A Manifesto

When I think about the possible evolutions of education still around the corner awaiting discovery, I am immediately challenged to look full circle at the scope of how far we've come. I can't help but marvel at the absolute permanent effects that have already been engendered throughout human society because of the recognition of the importance of education both as a formal and informal experience. As human beings, we learn constantly. Sometimes, our learning emerges out of reflection that was initiated by our navigation of carefully planned experiences. Sometimes, our learning is accidental and fresh from inspiration.

Nothing can deny that the experience of life is our primary teacher. It's hard to know how this happens as we, as a species, cannot decide on how experience even occurs. Possibly, there is a phantom objective reality which we, as Plato proposed, cannot become directly aware of, but which is utterly fascinating to the ghost in our machine, our soul. Or, perhaps there is no ghost in our machine or ultimate objective reality. Maybe all our magic, our human capacity both for good and evil, is inherent to the absolutely beautiful and interconnected structures of our brain.

In this case, the set of sensory stimulating impressions subjectively filtered into our ever burgeoning consciousness defines our movement through this life. Whatever is the case, there is no denying our human capacity to wonder about our world, our lives, and about each other. It's important to remember that all learning begins with this wonder.

Formal instruction, the thing that is typically called education, is the attempt to manufacture experience. This can be truly negative, if the experience is too tightly controlled for outcome. Releasing our preoccupation with outcome might be the wisest move for education to make. True only to its own rhythm, experience can unfurl slowly, unwrapping opportunity upon opportunity to glean understanding through disciplined observation or smack us with the delight of an epiphany. For education to evolve, attention has to be shifted to process.

Until that time when attention can shift to process, ideas that hint at ways for us to move forward, such as Gardner's Theory of Multiple Intelligences, will be stuck without much traction. Instead, the curriculum-centric models with their outcome biases will seek to use these inspirational learning theories as a way of trying to stuff more and more ideas into our heads, instead of challenging us to think better about what comes out of our mind.

In some instances, I'm sure that I sound negative about where the state of education is, as there are still so many pieces of this puzzle that are missing. There are still myriad hidden mysteries lurking within the human mind waiting for us. Currently, most of our theories about learning are still basically couched in ideational language. Our theories are beautiful stories that help us understand what seems to be happening when we learn, but cannot be completely articulated by the state of our understanding about how the brain develops. This is a huge challenge for anyone wanting to become cognizant about how humans learn.

At the same time, I have to recognize the beauty of how far

we've come. Keats once wrote that truth is beauty and beauty is truth. I suspect that his poetry was eerily prescient that the truth of how we learn will cause our entire species to marvel in the beauty that is life. Maybe this understanding will be enough to galvanize a new thinking about how an education should be developed. Without a doubt, I hope to live along this edge as I move through my adult career working to bring increasingly better educational experiences to those who wish to improve their lives through the pursuit of enlightenment. Truly, I cannot think of a nobler endeavor.

Considering the Western paradigm and history of intellectual thought, we have only enjoyed the widespread joy of reading and the influence that it has made for our society over the course of the last 500 years. If we look at this short time in the scope of all of human history, we have to marvel that there have never been so many literate human beings in the world at any time in the history of our species. Perhaps even more interesting is the thought that many of us live every minute of our days with ready access to the seminal ideas of the last 2500 years of human thought strewn about the Internet.

Even with the somewhat limited, but more textured access to information available through books, human beings have never been so awash in opportunities to learn from one another's experience. Again, it has always been mankind's capacity to tell stories and reflect on these stories which has defined much of what we consider to be culture.

It's easy to quickly point out that the concerted effort to print books over the course of the last 500 years, and to educate people to be able to access information from them, has fundamentally changed the way human beings think as individuals, behave among groups, and organize to accomplish the great goals of our existence that cannot be addressed in a solitary fashion.

Our successful existence in this day and age is defined by those projects which we decide warrant our effort. Our careers are a statement to eternity, not simply a pragmatic way to pay the bills and buy stuff. I say "stuff" here in a tongue-in-cheek manner as there is no substance for real and long-sighted motivation in its pursuit. We've learned that, as a species, each individual's voice is important and that each voice contributes to our path throughout time. Only as each of our voices overlap will the collective voice of humanity be heard. Furthermore, however cacophonous this voice might be, this is still our true and authentic voice. My decision to complete my doctoral degree, to reach the culmination of my education, was motivated by a desire to contribute my voice to the development of consciousness among our species.

I know many might laugh; truly, I recognize that this is a lofty goal. The capacity to contribute to the conversation about the place that education has in human society is, however, the food which nourishes me through the long nights of headache as I seek to, for example, save students from losing the motivation and bringing their own educational journey to a premature end. Those are the moments when a positive word from an esteemed mentor makes all the difference. My ability, however infinitesimally small, to affect the development of peoples' lives challenges me to fight through my own tiredness, laziness, and ever lurking malaise.

This recognition that I have a voice, however big or small, that can affect positive influence in peoples' lives buoys me as I struggle to allow my ideas to float onto the page, as I struggle to share my own stories.

The realities of education are evolving. With the advent of

books, we became no longer bound to the collective gatherings where long stories are shared which describe the ideas and lifestyles the participants conceive of as beautiful. Because of widespread literacy, we can learn these stories wherever we are, in the company of others or by ourselves.

This flexibility inherent to print media, books and now to an even more dizzyingly open degree with the Internet, has opened up the opportunity for multiple interpretations to every piece of truth shared among human beings since the era of oral tradition and spanning through to the very keystrokes creating this paragraph. Because it is not so easy to synthesize meaning in a collaborative group or craft an aesthetic through the codification of the seminal works of a culture, as education has moved away, ever so slightly, from being the ideological razor's edge of culture.

Each of the epochs of meaning transmission has strengths and weaknesses. As we gathered around a warm fire or a tree stump and shared stories, we developed a shared sense of meaning together. As our discussion evolved, we worked on a collaborative set of mores that helped us to define our communities and what we thought was important.

Such cultural artifacts as the roles of human beings as defined by age and gender, our spiritual sustenance, and how we might participate in our ecosystem in a balanced manner were important areas that inspired much collaborative reflection. In fact, I believe that there is probably an interesting correlation between this process of building shared and collaborative meaning, and the importance of balance with the environment, which is such a hallmark of societies which remained cohesive because of the dynamics of an oral tradition even through to the present day.

Books change the interactions among human beings

considerably. Each book might present the same story, the same truth, the same wisdom, but with a slightly different interpretation and with different vocabularies by the various writers who sought to share their perspective for a variety of different reasons. Each writer presented a new look at the piece of truth they wished to share with the world. With the dizzying amount of books published every year, the sheer amount of voices vying for attention became problematic for us as a society just beginning to learn about how literacy might affect our development. Two main developments became instantly and obviously needed: We needed people dedicated to reading books and schools to teach the skill of reading.

Besides just teaching us the skill of reading, the purpose of an education quickly became a lot more complex. Of course, some classes, especially those early in our education, focus specifically on allowing us to develop the vocabulary and basic analytical skills so that we might be able to cognitively handle the giants who have already come and left this world.

Others had a much more ideological purpose. We were introduced in a carefully planned and structured manner to idea after idea so as to better control the outcome of these experiences. While it only takes a few years to learn how to read, it is easy to recognize that schools have extended their mandate to also present to students those select books which are especially loud voices in human history.

In many ways, we are told what to believe and how to know what is true in a very different manner from that collaborative dynamic that was once an inherent part of our human societies during our participation in the oral tradition of ancient societies.

In some ways, we have come full circle in the time of the

Internet. We can now once again collaborate in meaning-making across vast distances, for example. At the same time, new challenges are presented. Anyone can upload anything onto the Internet without the editorial service provided by publishers or the authority of libraries to sanction a writer's presentation of truth as he or she sees it as seminal or to dismiss it as hogwash.

A successful education in this day and age is not so much about the content which is learned or by the modality in which this content is learned, but by careful mentorship in the access and conscious appraisal of information.

Separating the researcher from the subject and method of the research in my own experience, I can say that I understand and deeply appreciate my research participants' unanimous preference for the face to face traditional learning environment, but I cannot in good conscience dismiss what is happening to develop the online modality as what could possibly be the best way of improving society's access to quality education. My personal perspective is less about content or modality; instead, I focus this manifesto on the importance of relaying experience as a successful qualitative record of a life lived fully and consciously.

Sure, culture still has ideology. Education can and probably should still play a part in slicing away some perceived ugliness of the modern world if for no other reason than to better identify the parts of it which are truly beautiful and which, in the spirit of Keats, hint at truth; however, our collective consciousness as a species tells us that there is a limit to the lengths to which we should go to impress our findings on others. For example, no sane person should want to risk the annihilation of the planet just to prove a point about what he or she believes is good and beautiful. We've come too close to that precipice already.

Hopefully, as Nietzsche would point out, our staring into this abyss has shaken us as we came to realize the nothingness staring right back at us. Annihilation means nothing, proves nothing. Culture can no longer be bound with the idea that participation in rich face to face moments is the only way to soak meaning into our lives. Most importantly, competing cultures, in a world with the means to be destroyed, can no longer play win-lose or lose-lose strategies. Meaning permeates everything. Meaning is everywhere at all times. No one can know everything; we can simply prepare ourselves with the tools to grasp the meaning that we need when we need it. As educated people, sharing the great wisdom that transcends all borders and ethnic origins, we have to be looking for a path for the development of education that can be best described as inclusive, incisive, and progressive.

Any future of education that promotes our species' continual growth and development has to turn its attention to these visionary goals. Though unspecific and certainly not prescriptive, these three attributes offer us a cognitive zone to create shared values, an excellent thought location to begin the process of including the many perspectives and voices of our species. It is only through the active mentorship of critical thinking skills, in all of its varied appearances, and on a person by person basis, that we, as a species, can become more incisive and identify the way forward, not as a cohesive and united voice but as a deeply felt personal purpose.

There is no reason to continue if the motivation to do so does not well up from deep inside of us. If we feel included as valuable and trusted participants in our own development, then our motivation can be assured. Through this motivation, we are inspired to push ourselves along our own personal trajectories, to become more incisive versions of ourselves. Einstein said it many years ago when he pointed out that humanity's problems will never be solved at the same level of thinking as that which created the problem in the first place. We have to constantly strive for progression of consciousness, despite the reality that each solution will be a seed sowing the next challenge for mankind.

To this end, critical thinking skills should be the cohesive and culminating point of the time we spend as a student, at least from our late elementary through high school age education. And, in the spirit of Gardner's Theory of Multiple Intelligences which has informed this entire journey, we have to remember that critical thinking emerges through multiple means and in multiple thought-vocabularies.

Whether Gardner is right or whether his theory is another beautiful story that will eventually be relegated to the heap of anachronistic theories does not matter. Like a poem or quote which can fill a moment with meaning and help us to understand our paths through this life and our ways of interfacing with this world, the spirit of the theory is beautiful in that it challenges us to turn our focus away from the things we learn and the information that we collect, and focus on the experiences which inspire our minds to innovatively process creative new ways of handling the multifaceted challenges which continually arise in our personal lives and, by extension, in our efforts to participate actively in the family lives and careers which characterize our modern human societies, the voice of our times in the great stream of human history.

Our brains all sift through information in different ways. The best thing that we can do as educators is to encourage this active sifting as a driving motivation for living a conscious and successful human life. It matters not the learning environment which we use, as educators, to help students develop critical thinking. A learning environment is nothing but a tool. Tools do not create thoughtful masterpieces. Tools can do nothing without a vision; they cannot bring our inspiring visions to life. Visions, not tools, sculpt that which we find worthwhile, useful, and satisfying.

Our story comes full circle back to the words of the ancient Greek teacher, Socrates, who said that the unexamined life isn't worth living. Perhaps, the process of learning to ask incisive questions is more important than the answers that we arrive at.

It's fitting; I can't think of an easier way of staying motivated. I'm sure that I'm not alone in feeling my eyes shine when I feel a really interesting question begin to awaken inside of me. As a parting thought, I choose to playfully adopt poetic license and contend that Socrates was speaking to the ages to challenge us into continually developing our mind's ability to dig deeply into experience so that we can find the wisdom, truth and beauty awaiting us.

Zachary M. Oliver

Falling but Fulfilled

Zachary M. Oliver

Appendix

What is Intelligence?

Excerpt from "Multiple Intelligence & Learning Environments: An Investigation into Preferences and Predispositions"

A Dissertation by Zachary Oliver

Intellectual rigor is a prime concern of universities as they move to absorb online programs. The leaders of institutions are concerned that online learning environments are deficient at fostering learning and cannot effectively trigger intelligence. These leaders argue that learning is a social phenomenon. This widespread perspective is based on a long strand of philosophical thought, but is especially well-explored in the seminal work of Dewey that was established during the first half of the last century. Dewey's work had a huge influence on the American public school system. His central argument was that education should not only be a skill-based developmental process, but also a social environment that develops community and prepares individuals for citizenry (Andreasen, 2006).

Unfortunately, intelligence is neither the clearest nor best-defined concept. Much inquiry has been made throughout the history of western intellectualism. The topic demands a basic investigation of current thoughts, how these thoughts are theory-driven, what empirical evidence drives these theories, and what intellectual precursors germinated them. In order to have the research field come into focus, the history of modern thought needs examination to draw the connections clearly between the many disparate disciplines that have tangled with the question during just the last few hundred years.

A Brief History

When Descartes said "Cogito, ergo sum" about 400 years ago, he introduced a split between mind and brain from which modern intellectuals are still recovering. At the time, the split was necessary. Science, as a new intellectual discipline, was directly conflicting with the most powerful organization on Earth at the time: the Catholic Church. For an example of an early scientist who struggled in a civilization still dominated by Catholicism, Galileo was granted a lifetime of house arrest for his generosity to humanity: the demonstrable knowledge of a heliocentric galaxy. The observations of these early scientists were coming into direct conflict with Catholic dogma, as defined by architects of Christianity such as St. Thomas Aquinas (Appleyard, 1993).

Descartes carved the study of "epistemology" into two parts. Epistemology is defined as the study of knowledge and can be summed up in the questions: How do we know what we know? How is knowledge generated? Science claimed the observable elements of this world as its domain, while religion claimed the mystical or spiritual experience. This uneasy division has been the modern world's intellectual legacy implicit in Descartes' concept of Dualism (Appleyard, 1993).

Because observation has been the domain of science, conceptions about the observable reality of the physical world, for physical or social scientists, must evolve as the tools for observations evolve. These tools necessitate technology, which can be simply defined as the study of crafting and is practically defined through human tools (Kurzweil, 1999). The whole necessity of technology is implicit in this dynamic and discussed at length, for example, throughout sociology (Lipovetsky, 2005; Lyons, 1999; Postman, 1992).

The challenge to make an observation of intelligence has been very apparent at each step as the technologies used to make observations develop. Intelligence, perhaps more than any other concept, was ripped down the middle by dualism (Appleyard, 1993).

The question, at that time, was confusing: Was intelligence to be found in the physical brain or in the abstraction of the mind? The mind is fair game, after all, for the religious, or at least philosophical, because of its invisibility, while the brain, because of its physicality, remains in the domain of science. Later on, Darwin would shake the scientific and religious world violently with the introduction of his theory of evolution. Joined together with the philosophical ideas of Leibniz and Hobbes, the first modern definition of intelligence would be locked down as one concerned with computation (Pinker, 2002). Because of this specificity, this definition would hold huge sway throughout the literature even through to the present. In fact, it is still being hotly contested.

An early approach to intelligence testing was proposed by Sir Francis Galton, a cousin of Darwin. In 1869, just ten years after Darwin published his seminal text on evolution *Origin of the Species*, Galton published *Hereditary Genius*, which claimed that intelligence was a genetic trait, a biological technology passed down from person to person within families. He proposed, erroneously, that high levels of sensitivity, specifically measured by reaction time, to pressure on the skin was demonstrable intelligence, as was noticeably strong sight or hearing ability (Herrnstein & Murray, 1994). Galton's research shows that he was aware of the philosophical discussion of intelligence as a computational force.

During the first decade of the 1900's, a French scientist, Dr. Binet, was asked to try to measure intelligence in a new manner. Dr. Binet had no prior training in the field of intelligence and had very little from which to develop his measurements beyond the observations of his children, the literature left behind from Galton, as well as the various researchers of the Eugenics movement (Andreasen, 2006).

Despite Binet's disagreements with the way the test was adapted, most notably by Stanford professor Dr. Terman, into the Stanford-Binet scale, this was the birth of IQ.

For the last century, IQ has been the most accepted measurement of intelligence; this computational approach to measuring intelligence became ubiquitously accepted across the world as an objective measurement for human intelligence (Andreasen, 2006). Despite a few interesting rumblings from the community, most notably by Spearman's concept of "G," IQ's ubiquity was unchallenged. This acceptance, while a worthwhile compromise a hundred years ago, is hardly the "safe bet" that it once was (Pearce, 1992). The test has come against many challenges. It is found that different ethnic groups can score radically different on the Stanford-Binet IQ test, for example (Shuttleworth-Edwards, Kemp, Rust, Muirhead, Hartman, & Radloff, 2004). It is also found that multiple testing also apparently amplifies the IQ score (Flynn, 2007).

If the IQ score can be used to resurrect racial profiles (Herrnstein & Murray, 1994) or can be distorted through repeated examinations (Flynn, 2007), then the IQ test, as a measurement of intelligence, is ineffectual. This ineffectuality was based on the basic problem limiting science, the necessity for observable and replicable proof. IQ tests have been called a measurement of "computational skill" rather than intelligence, because the Stanford-Binet exam focuses on skills such as recognizing patterns (Woolley, 1992).

With the advent of cognitive psychology and the extremely dynamic disciplines collectively called neuroscience, conceptions of intelligence have drastically evolved. These disciplines no longer view the brain simply as a giant computational organ. Logic, while important, is not the sole summation of the myriad parts of the brain. The mind is no longer a spiritual abstraction. The mind is now considered, from empirical evidence, to be the self-conscious by-product of multiple parts of the brain working collectively and often layering on, interconnecting with, and redundantly supporting the other areas of the brain (De Bono, 1993; Kandel, 2006; Pearce, 1992).

Dr. Bruner was one of the first to articulate the shift away from purely computational definitions of intelligence in the field of education. It was his contention that human beings construct meaning through repeated exposure to the subject content in ever more complex ways (Ginsburg & Opper, 1969). While this isn't a definition of intelligence as a measurable quality, it does address something about how intelligence works. Intelligence can therefore be defined as a group of innate talents that work as parallel processes that we use to successfully construct meaning (Caine, R.

N. & Caine, G., 1994). After all, the skills necessary for participation in our post-modern society's milieu, sometimes called the Information Age, are based on the continual refinement of representations of reality by reinterpreting its elements (Knapp & Glenn, 1996).

At this point, even proponents of the computational approach accept that intelligence is far more involved than initially thought; the literature cites the computational superiority of computers juxtaposed with the scarcity of intelligence or consciousness of these same technological artifacts as proof (Kurzweil, 1999; Montague, 2006; Pinker, 2009; Woolley, 1992).

Researchers point out that advanced forms of computation may isolate particular value systems or be able to represent algorithmic thought processes. Unfortunately, this is not a simple solution. There still needs to be large amounts of simultaneous parallel processes incorporating vastly different kinds of computation in order for intelligence to be mimicked using technology. Intelligence is ready to be reassessed as a set of forces of the mind, rather than as a singular trait.

Multiple Intelligences: Theoretical Underpinning

The Theory of Multiple Intelligences (MI) comes out of the constructivist approach proposed by Jerome Bruner (Gardner, 1983). While Bruner felt that learning occurs best as students spiral through repeated experience, with ever-expanding difficulty, Gardner takes this idea one step further by adding that there are a few distinct applications of intelligences which help us to develop and encourage specialization (Armstrong, 2000; Barrington, 2004; Gardner, 1983; Gardner, 1999).

Both of these theorists belong to the constructivist theory, which "favors rich, authentic learning contexts over isolated decontextualized knowledge and skill" (Land & Hannafin, 2000, p. 8). By adding the special twists of specialization to Bruner's framework, Gardner proposed that student learning can be maximized across some specific learning styles that he consciously identified as "intelligences" (Shore, 2004; Silver, Strong, & Perini, 2000).

Gardner's use of the word "intelligence" was a deliberate choice that he discusses at length in his texts; he uses it because it more accurately describes the centrality of his ideas concerning human learning capacity. These intelligences, Gardner said after much research into neurophysiology and anatomy, are rooted in the biological functions of different areas of the brain (Gardner, 1999). Human beings specialize because of predispositions in their brains that come from a combination of genetics and environmental influences and become part of the way the brain functions (Caine, R. N. & Caine, G., 1994; Guild & Garger, 1998; Sprenger, 2003). In other words, these specializations have a biological foundation which has been reinforced in the day to day life of the individual.

These high functioning sections of the brain have been observed through neuroimaging and are linked with the neuroscientific concept of plasticity (Posner, 2004). Plasticity is the concept referring to the ability for synaptic connections to be continually reassessed and reset in the brain, which allows for a high degree of variability and specialization within the cerebral cortex, the area of the brain responsible for, among other things, perceptual experience (Kandel, 2006). This means that our perception of the world arises as synaptic connections are continually reinforced. Shifts are introduced when new connections are forged. Gardner (1999) posited that his theoretical framework for intelligence is rooted in this continually dynamic synaptic plasticity.

Learning, according to Gardner, is not conscious; it is intuitive (Denig, 2004). Gardner defined intelligence as "bio-psychological potential to process information that can be activated in a cultural setting that can be used to solve problems or create products that are of value in a culture" (Gardner, 1999, p. 33-34). In this definition, intelligence is not just computational ability; it is the ability to apply an understanding of something in a way that has "value" for a person or group of people as they interact with each other and with an environment that places demands on them (Diaz-Lefebvre, 2004).

These intelligences include: the Kinesthetic, Intrapersonal, Interpersonal, Naturalist, Linguistic, Visual-Spatial, Musical Intelligences, and Logical-Mathematical.

Gardner has continued to develop the ideas of MI along with a bevy of fellow educators. Many have advocated various activities and environments that can activate these intelligences. All researchers posit that every human being has all of the intelligences to a varying degree, but has typically also sought to specialize in one or two primary ones (Armstrong, 2000; Kallenbach & Viens, 2001).

The theory has been commonly applied to acting as a practical approach to devising small scale activities designed to stimulate cognition within a diverse environment of learners. Instead of limiting the application of this theory to the creation of more and more classroom strategies designed to fill students with more and more information, allowing it to voice an alternative to our perspective about how we can create effective learning environments that speak to our capacity for intelligence in all its forms, The theory also allows us to move forward cognizant of what we need in order to fulfill our individual potential and the potential of our children.

Elliot Eisner (2004) has provided an excellent article on the matter. In this article, he examines multiple intelligences, especially as to how this theory affects our thinking about educational reform. Relying on years of experience rather than hard scientific research, Eisner mentions that it seems somehow intuitive that not all students learn the same way and with the same proclivities.

This attitude seems to be an outcropping of his educational connoisseurship evaluation model developed much earlier from the rich personalized observations Eisner made at a time when qualitative research methodology was becoming codified (Marsh & Willis, 2006). Eisner reasons that a standardized curriculum is the worst method with which education, as a field of professionals, can address the shortcomings of an education system. Yet, it is the defining benchmark of all publicly funded elementary and secondary schools across America and of our entire accreditation system in higher education. Federal funding is strategically placed in those schools which meet strict standard benchmarks.

Furthermore, as education becomes more and more mechanized into online learning environments to meet the challenging constraints of non-traditional learners, the impulse is to move more and more towards a content-heavy curriculum-centered approach.

Technology

The research of computer-based learning environments and multiple intelligence theory has become widespread during the last decade. In fact, the literature abounds with examples of how and why technology and multiple intelligences are a natural fit (Alessi & Trollip, 2001; Bocchi, Eastman, & Swift, 2004; Dabbagh & Bannan-Ritland, 2005; Gardner, 1999; Hoefling, 2003; Shelly, Cashman, Gunter, R. E. & Gunter, G. A., 2004; Simonson, Smaldino, Albright, & Zvacek, 2002).

The strongest argument offered is that multiple representations of material are better facilitated by using technological means that release the focus of control from the instructor and place it firmly into the hands of the learner (Jonassen, Howland, Moore, & Marra, 2003).

Self-efficacy is the underlining buzzword throughout the literature about technological synthesis with education (Richardson & Newby, 2006). There are volumes of activities and rationale that attest to the idea that these two theories may provide a synergistic environment that generates more self-efficacy, higher-order thinking skills, and a superlative active learning cognitive environment (Jonassen et al., 2003; Merrill, Hammons, Vincent, Reynolds, Christensen, & Tolman, 1996; Thorsen, 2003).

The most important consideration, though, is that improvements in learning can never be specifically recognized as stemming solely from a new technology (Bruning, Schraw, Norby, & Ronning, 2004; Kearsley, 2004).

On one hand, technology is made to be the key new component in the restructuring of the education system because, among other reasons, well-implemented technology promises to create learning environments that are more active (Knapp & Glenn, 1996). When considering all of the programs commercially available and the continually growing databases on the Internet, the personal computer, the main expression of high technology in education, gives teachers and students a vast repository of information that can be accessed at any time from multiple interfaces and through parallel pathways (Thorsen, 2003).

Computers can be used to function as platforms for interactive coursework to challenge students to think their way through obstacles, as well as to articulate how and why choices were made (Knapp & Glenn, 1996). It has been said that this context and content-rich atmosphere is extremely successful both in activating cognitive skills as well as in engaging intrinsic motivation (Tomei, 2002).

The important distinction to make, however, is that the computer cannot be developed into the mold of a teacher; this is not its purpose. It does not make students learn; rather, the computer, when developed with the correct software and presented at the proper moment in the learning process, presents information and offers an opportunity for students to make new connections to a subject matter in such a way that the student is challenged to think (Bruning et al., 2004; Jonassen et al., 2003; Knapp & Glenn, 1996; Tomei (2002). The dynamic hinted at by this description is not, by any means, social. The picture it describes is of a student hunkered away quietly alternating between clicks of a mouse and pecks at a keyboard. The whole structure of social learning and community has to be re-imagined in the face of these technological additions into our learning environments.

Lyons warns that meaning loses boundaries in a persistent environment of technology because the structure of community disappears (1999). Technology undermines community because it infiltrates and structures the way information and communication flows. The technology that develops within the boundaries of a community or system is an inherent part of the ideology of that system. Boundaries of a community or system are developed along ideological lines (Berger & Luckmann, 1967). If ideology is subverted, then the identity of the community is also corrupted.

Human community, while replete with myriad definitions, is a direct experience; it is shared among people that have the same aim, purposes, and fate (Keller, 2003). If a computer is introduced to mediate community, then the flow of communication through the community can only run through the protocols set up within that technology. Technology then mediates the community (Baudrillard, 1994). In other words, technology carries with it an ideological bias of its own (Postman, 1992). It seems that the predilection to move towards a curriculum-centric model is indicative of this bias.

Whether positive or negative, technology specifically connects to the topic at hand as that set of special tools that allows a student to study from a distance with no constraints of time or place.

Learning Environments and Communities

Community forms around bonds of shared meaning and concern in order to continually support its own development through the continued conscious evolution of shared ideas and concepts (Keller, 2003; Lee, 2006; Morgan, Rawlinson, & Weaver, 2006). It has been theorized that human beings do this because groups have a better survival rate than individuals. The energy of decision making, when put into the hands of many working with a shared ideology, seems to have more coherence and to be better articulated (Surowiecki, 2004).

Also, by participating in community, individuals have a greater ability to specialize. Community breeds cooperation, and when cooperation is codified by a community, individuals within the system have the cohesive synergy of shared definitions, values, and conceptual frameworks, which they can implement to move towards a more diversified system while simultaneously developing a formalized method of dealing with forces and entities outside the system. Systems theory, as defined by Luhmann, has punctuated this by saying that a system develops through the process of understanding the environment which it inhabits (Moeller, 2006). Humanity seeks to understand the world which we inhabit through all of our various and combined efforts. We lend our voices to careers that explore various environments, whether that environment is financial, social, or biological. In turn, we generate huge amounts of knowledge about these various areas that contribute to future efforts and the development of our entire system of humanity.

While the specialization-diversity dynamic within a system sounds desirable, community, and the context governing it, can be constraining. Philosophers are quick to point this out by indicating the enormous pressures that social constraints place on individuals within a system. Diversity within a system seems to strain the performance of individuals operating within its boundaries. The literature shows that in some instances difficult tasks become more difficult, from a perceptual perspective, when other individuals are watching. It also shows that easy tasks show higher accuracy when observed (Plous, 1993). This seems to be evidence of the conforming force that social interactions have on individuals in groups. The easy tasks are easy because they are mundane and within the easy norm of the group. These actions do not draw attention and therefore do not endanger the individual performing them to come under the scrutiny of the ideology.

This is the point at which education enters the frame. Education is the process by which meaning is conveyed, whether formally or informally (Keirns, 1999) and has been called a conforming force (Krishnamurti, 1953). Education is the primary tool from which systems are generated. Education has a strong social context and is linked with the formation and perpetuation of systems or groups of people through the development of what Dewey called character (Goble, 1970).

Learning environments are linked with education. Typically the term is used to refer to the formalized place in which conscious education, also called instruction, occurs. Instruction, according to the literature, operates on two fundamental principles: learning must be consciously focused on a predetermined course and it must be evaluated against an existing benchmark (Keirns, 1999). Likewise, learning environments are places designed to meet specific educational goals (Sargeant, Curran, Allen, Jarvis-Selinger, & Ho, 2006). The challenge is that learning environments become the vortex around which community forms, ideology grows, and where social networks are formed (Wenger, 1998). The concern is whether, in the midst of all of these external influences, there is any place left for the growth of identity and the intelligence which supports each individual's active participation in this world.

References

1) Alessi, S. M. & Trollip, S. R. (2001). *Multimedia for learning: Methods and development* (3rd Ed.). Boston: Allyn & Bacon.
2) Andreasen, N. C. (2006). *The creative brain: The science of genius*. New York: Plume Books.
3) Appleyard, B. (1993). *Understanding the present: Science and the soul of modern man*. New York: Anchor Books.
4) Armstrong, T. (2000). *Multiple intelligences in the classroom*. Alexandria: Association for Supervision and Curriculum Development.
5) Barrington, E. (2004). Teaching to student diversity in higher education: How multiple intelligence theory can help. *Teaching in Higher Education 9*(4), 421-434.
6) Baudrillard, J. (1994). *Simulacra and simulation*. Ann Arbor: University of Michigan Press.
7) Berger, P. & Luckmann, T. (1967). *The social construction of reality: A treatise on the sociology of knowledge*. New York: Doubleday.
8) Bocchi, J., Eastman, J. K., & Swi*ft, C. O. (2004). Retaining the online learner: Profile of students in an* online MBA program and implications for teaching them. *Journal of Education for Business 79*(4), 245-253.
9) Brunning, R. H., Schraw, G. J., Norby, M. M., & Ronning, R. R. (2004). *Cognitive psychology and instructio*n (4th Ed.). Upper Saddle River: Pearson Education, Inc.
10) Caine, R. N. & Caine, G. (1994). *Making connections: Teaching and the human brain*. Menlo Park: Dale Seymour Publications, Inc.
11) Dabbagh, N. & Bannan-Ritland, B. (2005). *Online learning:*

Concepts, strategies, and application. Upper Saddle River: Pearson Education, Inc.

12) Davis, L. (2004). *Using the theory of multiple intelligences to increase fourth-grade students' academic achievement in science* (Doctoral Dissertation). Retrieved on August 1, 2007 from ERIC database

13) De Bono, E. (1993). *Serious creativity: Using the power of lateral thinking to create new ideas.* New York: HarperBusiness.

14) Denig, S. J. (2004). Multiple intelligence and learning styles: Two complementary dimensions. *Teachers College Record 106* (1), 96-111.

15) Diaz-Lefebvre, R. (2004). Multiple intelligences, learning for understanding, and creative assessment: Some pieces to the puzzle of learning. *Teachers College Record 106*(1), 49-57.

16) Eisner, E. W. (2004). *The arts and the creation of mind.* New Haven: Yale University Press.

17) Flynn, J. R. (2007). Solving the IQ puzzle. *Scientific American Mind 18*(5), 24-31.

18) Gardner, H. (1983). *Frames of mind.* New York: Basic Books Inc.

19) Gardner, H. (1999). *Intelligence reframed.* New York: Basic Books Inc.

20) Ginsburg, H. & Opper, S. (1969). *Piaget's theory of intellectual development: An introduction.* Englewood Cliffs: Prentice-Hall, Inc.

21) Goble, F. G. (1970). *The third force: The psychology of Abraham Maslow.* New York: Simon & Schuster, Inc.

22) Guild, P. B. & Garger, S. (1998). *Marching to different drummers* (2nd ed.). Alexandria: Association for Supervision

and Curriculum Development.

23) Herrnstein, R. J. & Murray, C. (1994). *The bell curve: Intelligence and class structure in American life.* New York: Simon & Schuster Inc.

24) Hoefling, T. (2003). *Working virtually: Managing people for successful virtual teams and organizations.* Sterling: Stylus Publishing, LLC.

25) Jonassen, D. H. & Land, S. M. (2000). *Theoretical foundations of learning environments.* Mahwah: Lawrence Erlbaum Associates, Inc., Publishers.

26) Kallenbach, S. & Viens, J. (2001). *Multiple intelligences in practice: Teacher research reports from multiple intelligences study.* Boston: World Education.

27) Kandel, E. R. (2006). *In search of memory: The emergence of a new science of mind.* New York: W.W. Norton & Company, Inc.

28) Keller, S. (2003). *Community: Pursuing the dream, living the reality.* Princeton: Princeton University Press.

29) Kearsley, G. (2004). *Online education: Learning and teaching in cyberspace.* Belmont: Wadsworth Group.

30) Keirns, J. L. (1999). *Designs for self-instruction: Principles, processes, and issues in developing self-directed learning.* Needham Heights: Allyn & Bacon.

31) Knapp, L. R., & Glenn, A. D. (1996). *Restructuring schools with technology.* Upper Saddle River: A Pearson Education Company.

32) Krishnamurti, J. (1953). *Education & the significance of life.* New York: HarperCollins.

33) Kurzweil, R. (1999). *The age of spiritual machines.* New York: Penguin Books.

34) Land, S. M. & Hannafin, M. J. (2000). Student-centered learning environments. In D. H. Jonassen & S. M. Land (Ed.), *Theoretical foundations of learning environments* (pp. 1-24) Mahwah: Lawrence Erlbaum Associates, Inc., Publishers.

35) Lee, K.-T. (2006). Online learning in primary schools: Designing for school culture change. *Educational Media International 43*(2), 91-106.

36) Lipovetsky, G. (2005). *Hypermodern times*. Malden: Polity Press.

37) Lyons, D. (1999). *Postmodernity*. Minneapolis: University of Minnesota Press.

38) McKinney, K. (2007). Active learning (Online database). Retrieved on October 22, 2007 from: http://www.teachtech.ilstu.edu/additional/tips/newActive.php

39) Merrill, P. F., Hammons, K., Vincent, B. R., Reynolds, P. L., Christensen, L., & Tolman, M. N. (1996). *Computers in education*. Needham Heights: Allyn & Bacon.

40) Moeller, H. (2006). *Luhmann explained: From souls to systems*. Peru: Carus Publishing Company.

41) Montague, R. (2006). *Why choose this book?* New York: The Penguin Group.

42) Morgan, J., Rawlinson, M., & Weaver, M. (2006). Facilitating online reflective learning for health and social care professionals. *Open Learning 21*(2), 167-176.

43) Pearce, J. C. (1992). *Evolution's end: Claiming the potential of our intelligence*. New York: HarperCollins.

44) Pinker, S. (2002). The blank slate: The modern denial of human nature. New York: Penguin Books.

45) Pinker, S. (2009). *How the mind works*. New York: W. W.

Norton & Company, Inc.

46) Plous, S. (1993). *The psychology of judgment and decision making*. New York: McGraw-Hill, Inc.

47) Posner, M. (2004). Neural systems and individual differences. *Teachers College Record 106*(1), 24-30.

48) Postman, N. (1992). *Technopoly: The surrender of culture to technology*. New York: Vintage Books USA.

49) Rawson, H. & Miner, M. (Ed.). (1986). *The new international dictionary of quotations*. New York: A Mentor Book.

50) Richardson, J. C. & Newby, T. (2006). The role of students' cognitive engagement in online learning. *American Journal of Distance Education 20*(1), 23-37.

51) Sargeant, J., Curran, V., Allen, M., Jarvis-Selinger, S., & Ho, K. (2006). Facilitating interpersonal interaction and learning online: Linking theory and practice. *Journal of Continuing Education in the Health Professions 26*(2), 128-136.

52) Shelly, G.B., Cashman, T.J., Gunter, R.E. & Gunter, G.A. (2004). *Teachers discovering computers: Integrating technology into the classroom*. Boston: Thomson Course Technology.

53) Shore, J. R. (2004). Teacher education and multiple intelligences: A case study of multiple intelligences and teacher efficacy in two teacher preparation courses. *Teachers College Record 106*(1), 112-139.

54) Shuttleworth-Edwards, A. B., Kemp, R. D., Rust, A. L., Muirhead, J. G. L., Hartman, N. P., & Radloff, S. E. (2004). Cross-cultural effects on IQ test performance: A review and preliminary normative indications on WAIS-III test performance. *Journal of Clinical & Experimental Neuropsychology 26*(7), 903-921.

55) Simonson, M., Smaldino, S., Albright, M., & Zvacek, S. (2002). *Teaching and learning at a distance: Foundations of distance education* (2nd ed.). Upper Saddle River: Prentice Hall.
56) Silver, H. F., Strong, R. W., & Perini, M. J. (2000). *So each may learn: Integrating learning styles & multiple intelligences*. Alexandria: Silver Strong & Associates, Inc.
57) Sprenger, M. (2003). *Differentiation through learning styles and memory*. Thousand Oaks: Corwin Press, Inc.
58) Surowiecki, J. (2004). *The wisdom of crowds: Why the many are smarter than the few and how collective wisdom shapes business, economies, societies, and nations*. New York: Doubleday.
59) . Thorsen, C. (2003). *TechTactics: Instructional models for educational computing*. Boston: Pearson Education Inc.
60) Tomei, L. A. (2002). *The technology façade: overcoming barriers to effective instructional technology*. Boston: Allyn & Bacon.
61) Wenger, E. (1998). *Communities of practice: Learning, meaning, and identity*. New York: Cambridge University Press.
62) Woolley, B. (1992). *Virtual worlds*. New York: Penguin Books.

Zachary M. Oliver

Falling but Fulfilled

About the Author

Zachary Oliver continually searches for his ideal: balance. Originally from Vienna, Austria, a center for old European culture, he has chosen Honolulu, Hawaii, arguably the most geographically remote place on Earth to live and write. He has recently found his calling as an individual comfortably balancing the identity of a scholar-practitioner and as a leader of organizations that work to develop interested learners into successful professionals.

He is the editor of *First Breath—2010 Savant Anthology of Poems* (Savant 2010).

Zachary M. Oliver (Editor)
72 pp. 8.25" x 5" Softcover
ISBN 978-0-9845552-2-2

Twenty-nine poems by ten outstanding poets and writers selected by Zachary M. Oliver for their outstanding merit. Contributors include Helen Doan, Erin L. George, Jack Howard, Daniel S. Janik, Scott Mastro, Zachary M. Oliver, Francis H. Powell, Gabjirel Ra, V. Bright Saigal and Orest Stocco.

If you enjoyed *Falling but Fulfilled* consider these other fine Books from Savant Books and Publications:

Dare to Love in Oz by William Maltese

A Whale's Tale by Daniel S. Janik
Tropic of California by R. Page Kaufman
The Village Curtain by Tony Tame
The Interzone by Tatsuyuki Kobayashi
Today I Am A Man by Larry Rodness
The Bahrain Conspiracy by Bentley Gates
Called Home by Gloria Schumann
Kanaka Blues by Mike Farris
Poor Rich by Jean Blasiar
First Breath: 2010 Savant Anthology of Poems, edited by Zachary Oliver
The Jumper Chronicles by W. C. Peever
My Unborn Child by Orest Stocco
Last Song of the Whales by Four Arrows
Perilous Panacea by Ronald Klueh

Scheduled for Release in 2010:
Mythical Voyage by Robin Ymer
Ammon's Horn by Guerrino Amati
Charlie No Face by David Seaburn
Hello, Norma Jean by Sue Dolleris
In Dire Straits by Jim Currie
In the Himalayan Nights by Anoop Chandola
Still Life with Cat and Mouse by Sheila McGraw
Manifest Intent by Mike Farris
Richer by Jean Blasiar
Number One Bestseller by Brian Morley
Blood Money by Scott Mastro

http://www.savantbooksandpublications.com

Made in the USA
Charleston, SC
09 July 2012